Campaign

MW01044736

PREY
SHING

Anzio 1944

The beleaguered beachhead

Campaign · 155

Anzio 1944

The beleaguered beachhead

Steven J Zaloga · Illustrated by Peter Dennis
Series editor Lee Johnson

First published in 2005 by Osprey Publishing
Midland House, West Way, Botley, Oxford OX2 0PH, UK
443 Park Avenue South, New York, NY 10016, USA
E-mail: info@ospreypublishing.com

© 2005 Osprey Publishing Limited

All rights reserved. Apart from any fair dealing for the purpose of private study,
research, criticism or review, as permitted under the Copyright, Designs and
Patents Act, 1988, no part of this publication may be reproduced, stored in a
retrieval system, or transmitted in any form or by any means, electronic,
electrical, chemical, mechanical, optical, photocopying, recording or otherwise,
without the prior written permission of the copyright owner. Enquiries should be
addressed to the Publishers.

A CIP catalog record for this book is available from the British Library

ISBN 1 84176 9134

Design: The Black Spot
Index by Fineline Editorial Services
3D bird's-eye views by The Black Spot
Battlescene artwork by Peter Dennis
Originated by Grasmere Digital Imaging, Leeds, UK
Printed in China through World Print Ltd.

05 06 07 08 09   10 9 8 7 6 5 4 3 2 1

For a catalog of all books published by Osprey please contact:

NORTH AMERICA
Osprey Direct, 2427 Bond Street, University Park, IL 60466, USA
E-mail: info@ospreydirectusa.com

ALL OTHER REGIONS
Osprey Direct UK, P.O. Box 140 Wellingborough, Northants, NN8 2FA, UK
E-mail: info@ospreydirect.co.uk

www.ospreypublishing.com

Author's Note

The author would like to thank the staff of the US Army's
Military History Institute (MHI) at the Army War College at
Carlisle Barracks, PA and the staff of the US National
Archive, College Park for their kind assistance in the
preparation of this book. Thanks also go to Norman
Friedman for help on this project.

For brevity, the traditional conventions have been used
when referring to units. In the case of US units, 1/179th
Infantry refers to the 1st Battalion, 179th Infantry Regiment.
In the case of German units, 1/Panzer Regiment 7 refers to
the 1st Battalion, Panzer Regiment 7; GR 725 indicates
Grenadier Regiment 725.

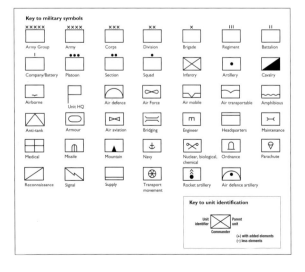

CONTENTS

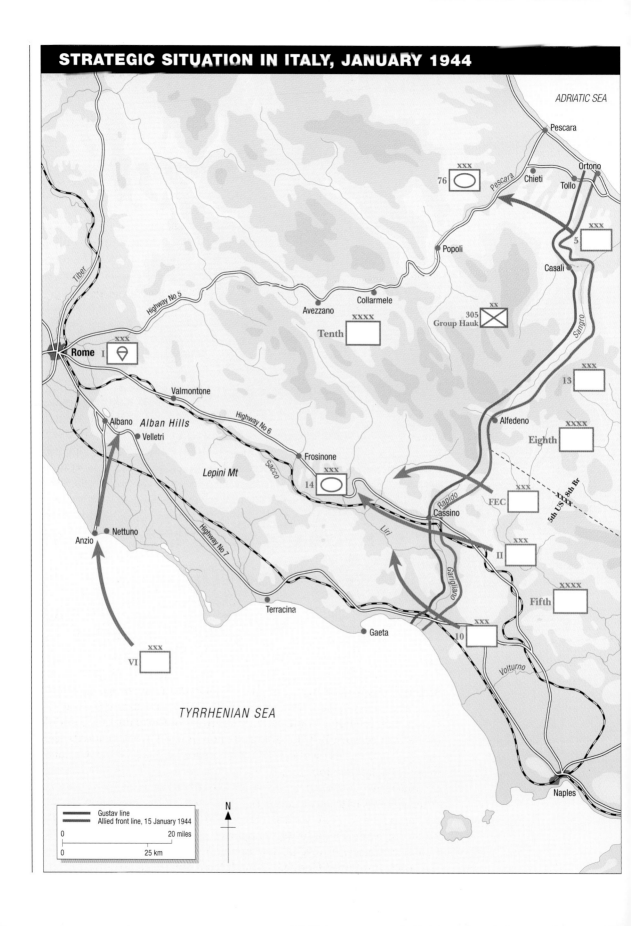

STRATEGIC SITUATION IN ITALY, JANUARY 1944

ADRIATIC SEA

Pescara

Ortono

76 XXX

Chieti

Tollo

5 XXX

Popoli

Casali

Tiber

Highway No 5

Collarmele

Avezzano

Tenth XXXX

305 Group Hauk XX

Sangro

Rome I XXX

13 XXX

Valmontone

Albano Alban Hills

Velletri

Highway No 6

Alfedeno

Eighth XXXX

5th US XX 8th Br

Lepini Mt

Sacco

Frosinone

14 XXX

Rapido

FEC XXX

Anzio

Nettuno

Highway No 7

Liri

Cassino

II XXX

Garigliano

Fifth XXXX

VI XXX

Terracina

Gaeta

10 XXX

Volturno

TYRRHENIAN SEA

Naples

N

Gustav line
Allied front line, 15 January 1944

0   20 miles
0   25 km

ORIGINS OF THE BATTLE

The Anzio amphibious landing of 1944 was one of the most controversial Allied operations in Europe in World War II. Although intended to break the stalemate in the Italian theater by making an end run around the German Gustav line defenses near Cassino, instead Anzio itself became a stalemate. Churchill famously remarked, "We hoped to land a wildcat that would tear out the bowels of the Boche. Instead, we have stranded a vast whale." The Anzio operation presents a classic study of ambitious political objectives doomed by limited military resources. Grim memories of the nearly disastrous Salerno landings haunted the Allied commanders, and instead of a bold advance after the initial landing in January 1944, they consolidated the beachhead to await the inevitable German counter attack. The beachhead survived three violent attacks in February, the largest German counter attacks in the west until the Ardennes offensive ten months later. By March, Anzio had degenerated into an agonizing stalemate. Ironically, an operation that had been launched to redeem the Gustav line operation in the end depended on a successful conclusion of the Cassino breakthrough before the bridgehead could be exploited. To further add to the controversy of the operation, Gen Mark Clark decided to focus the advance out of Anzio in the direction of Rome rather than eastward to trap the German forces retreating from the Cassino sector. Rome fell to the Allies on 4 June 1944, but it was a bitter victory that was quickly forgotten when the main Allied campaign opened in Normandy two days later.

THE STRATEGIC SETTING

At the heart of the Anzio controversy was the divergent strategic perspectives of the British and American allies. For Churchill, the Mediterranean was the "carotid artery of Empire", the key access route to Egypt, the Middle East, and ultimately to India. Military operations in the Mediterranean were historically well suited to British proclivities for a peripheral engagement strategy when dealing with a strong continental power such as France in the early 19th century or Germany in the middle of the 20th century. British power rested on its naval strength and its army was too small on its own to overcome a major land power like Germany in direct confrontation. As a result, Britain preferred to use the leverage of maritime mobility to extract maximum results from modest commitments of ground forces. Britain depended on a coalition strategy for the final end-game against a land power such as Germany, but in the mid-term, a peripheral strategy supported this objective. In the case of the Italian campaign, Churchill saw operations as serving several essential purposes. It drew off German strength from the Russian front, providing aid and comfort to the beleaguered Red Army. The commitment of army resources was not particularly extensive, and indeed much of the manpower in the Italian campaign came from the colonies, including Canada, South Africa, India, and New Zealand. The Mediterranean theater played on British strengths, especially the well established Royal Navy presence, and exploited Axis weaknesses, especially the vulnerability of the Italians.

The American perspective was significantly different. Since the US was fighting a two-front war in both the Atlantic and the Pacific, American leaders were not keen on wasting resources in secondary theaters. The US Army chief of staff, George C. Marshall, saw the primary aim of the campaign in Europe to be the defeat of Germany. Marshall was unconvinced by Churchill's depiction of the Mediterranean as representing "the soft underbelly of Europe" and considered Churchill's preference for Mediterranean operations to be a "prestige" venture that was strategically unsound. Marshall wanted a direct confrontation with Germany as soon as possible on the most feasible battleground, namely an invasion of northern France. Any other operations were merely distractions from the main goal. From a political perspective, the United States had little reason to support British imperial ambitions, and indeed there was a strong anti-imperial strain in US foreign policy both before and after World War II that was only partly suppressed for the sake of the coalition during the war.

Ultimately, Churchill managed to win over Roosevelt to Mediterranean operations in 1942–43. The Allies were not yet ready to land in France as was all too clear from the performance of the inexperienced US Army in Tunisia in 1942–43. Roosevelt recognized that it was essential to keep Russia in the war on the Allied side, and Stalin was insisting on a second front. The Mediterranean theater offered the prospect of morale-boosting victories on the cheap since Italy was clearly vulnerable. Furthermore, Hitler seemed willing to take the bait and waste significant forces in the theater even if it was a strategic dead end for Germany.

Although Churchill had won Roosevelt's acquiescence to continued Allied operations in the Mediterranean in the winter of 1943–44, the US support was not unconditional. The US was not willing to devote substantial naval or army resources to the theater since critical operations in both Europe and the Pacific were expected in the summer of 1944. At every turn, Allied commanders in Italy would have to beg for every last battalion, every last landing craft, and every last fighter plane. Their only leverage was the prospect of liberating Rome. Both Churchill and Roosevelt recognized the political importance of seizing a major Axis capital, and Rome would certainly do even though Mussolini had been forced out of the war in September 1943 after the Salerno landings. The lure of Rome helped extract a few extra resources for the Italian theater in spite of growing US impatience.

If British and American differences in strategic outlooks set the broad parameters for operations in Italy, combat experiences in 1943 helped shape the operational setting. The Mediterranean theater might seem like the soft underbelly of Europe on a map, but it did not seem that way to Allied army units involved in the fighting in 1943. Campaigns in Italy are inevitably dominated by the Italian geography, especially the

US infantry practice amphibious landings near Pozzuoli in early January in anticipation of Operation *Shingle*. (NARA)

Apennine mountain chain which form the spine of the Italian peninsula in the center. The narrow coastal plains offered the Allies little room to maneuver, and as a result, the fighting in Italy in the autumn and winter of 1943 inevitably involved bitter infantry fighting to overcome determined German defenses in the foothills and mountains. This became all too clear when the Allied advance bogged down along the Gustav defensive line in front of Cassino on the western side of the Apennines and in front of Ortona on the eastern side. The obvious solution to this dilemma was an amphibious operation, exploiting the Allies' naval superiority to shift forces around the German defenses as had been done in September 1943 at Salerno. The US Fifth Army commander, Gen Mark Clark, had set up a special staff within his G-3 (operations) department in October 1943 specifically to look for amphibious landing opportunities.

While there was little question that an amphibious operation was the solution to the stalemate in front of the Gustav line, there was the overriding issue of naval resources. A total of 90 LSTs (landing ship, tank) were available in the Mediterranean in the autumn of 1943 after the Salerno landings and they were being used to move troops and supplies from North Africa and Sicily into Italy. However, in preparation for Operation *Overlord* (Normandy) and Operation *Anvil* (southern France) scheduled for May 1944, 68 of these ships were scheduled to depart in mid-December 1943 for their new assignment. A similar situation affected other necessary equipment for amphibious operations such as landing craft, DUKW amphibious trucks and other equipment. Any amphibious operation in Italy would have to be undertaken soon and with limited resources.

CHRONOLOGY

8 November 1943 – Alexander outlines mission to Clark of an amphibious landing to outflank the Gustav line, starting the planning process

25 November 1943 – Plan for Operation *Shingle* is presented to Gen Alexander by Fifth Army G-3

10 December 1943 – Clark suggests revision of Operation *Shingle*, enlarging the landing force

22 December 1943 – Operation *Shingle* canceled due to failure of Fifth Army to advance past Cassino

25 December 1943 – Churchill resurrects Operation *Shingle* as a means to revive the flagging fortunes of the Italian campaign

21 January 1944 – Task Force 81 departs ports in Naples area for Anzio

0200 hours, 22 January 1944 – Pre-landing bombardment of Anzio beaches begins, first landings follow

0500 hours, 22 January 1944 – Kesselring receives first news of landings, activates Case Richard, the reinforcement plan

25 January 1944 – First skirmishing along Anzio perimeter, mainly around Aprilia

Midnight, 30 – 31 January 1944 – Allies begin first attack out of beachhead

31 January 1944 - British infantry secure Campoleone, but US advance on Cisterna falters after two Ranger battalions are trapped

Night, 3 – 4 February 1944 – German 14th Army launches first major counter-offensive aimed at securing Campoleone from the British 1st Division. Attacks force withdrawal to "The Factory"

Night, 7 – 8 February 1944 – German 14th Army renews attacks down Via Anziate towards "The Factory", starting a four day battle for Aprilia

11 February 1944 – US 45th Division attempts to retake "The Factory" from the Germans but after a see saw battle, "The Factory" remains in German hands

Dawn, 16 February 1944 – Operation *Fischfang* starts, aimed at dividing the beachhead in two along the Via Anziate. Intense but inconclusive fighting rages for three days

19 February 1944 – German attacks peter out, marking the end of Operation *Fischfang*

22 February 1944 – Gen John Lucas, VI Corps commander, relieved of command. Gen Lucian Truscott takes over command of the Anzio beachhead

Dawn, 29 February 1944 – Operation *Seitensprung* begins, a renewed attempt to secure the Via Anziate. The attack quickly falters in the face of withering Allied artillery firepower

Evening, 1 March 1944 – In the wake of the failure of Operation *Seitensprung*, Kesselring orders 14th Army over to the defensive. Mackensen begins to shift units away from the beachhead for rest and rebuilding

March – April 1944 – The "Big war of little battles" ensues due to the stalemate on the Anzio beachhead. Both sides stage raids and artillery duels, but no major attacks take place

11 May 1944 – Operation *Diadem* starts with a combined assault by the US Fifth Army and the British Eighth Army against the Gustav line

17 May 1944 – The monastery at Monte Cassino is finally taken, marking the rupture of the Gustav line. The German 10th Army is in retreat from the Gustav line towards Rome

Dawn, 23 May 1944 – Operation *Buffalo* is launched from the Anzio beachhead, aimed at the Velletri gap

26 May 1944 – With the VI Corps firmly in the foothills of the Alban hills, Clark decides to shift the emphasis from the Cassino–Rome highway to a direct northward assault towards Rome

Evening, 30 May 1944 – After encountering stiff German resistance along the Caesar line, the 36th Division infiltrates two regiments into the Alban hills, outflanking the German defenses

Evening, 2 June 1944 – With his forces outflanked by the US penetration through the Alban hills, Mackensen orders a general withdrawal from the Caesar line past Rome.

Morning, 4 June 1944 – Reconnaissance elements of VI Corps reach suburbs of Rome

Afternoon, 4 June 1944 – Major units of the VI Corps including the 1st Armored Division and 36th Division enter Rome

5 June 1944 – Rome is secured

OPPOSING COMMANDERS

GERMAN COMMANDERS

Generalfeldmarschall Albert Kesselring, served as OB Südwest (Commander-in-Chief Southwest) as well as commander of Army Group C.

Generaloberst Eberhard von Mackensen, commander of the German 14th Army, seen here after the war. (NARA)

The senior German commander in Italy was Generalfeldmarschall Albert Kesselring, who served as Oberbefehlshaber Südwest (Commander-in-Chief Southwest), a slight change in title that came into effect on 21 November 1943. Kesselring had previously been the OB-Süd during the North African campaign and during the initial phase of the Italian campaign. This command was oriented towards the defense of southern Italy while a separate Army Group B command, under Generalfeldmarschall Erwin Rommel since the summer of 1943, was responsible for defense of northern Italy and the Appennines. When Rommel's headquarters was transferred to France in late 1943 in preparation for the expected Allied invasion of France in 1944, Kesselring's command was reconfigured to control the defense of all of Italy, as well as the Adriatic Coastal Region (Slovenia). Kesselring had tactical authority over all German military units in Italy, including the Luftwaffe and Kriegsmarine, though both the air force and navy commanders in Italy nominally reported to their service commanders in Berlin. During the November 1943 command changes in Italy, a new Army Group C headquarters was created to control the 10th and 14th Armies, and Kesselring served as its head as well as his OB-Südwest post.

Kesselring was an unusual figure in such a senior command post, as he was a Luftwaffe officer, not an army officer. Nevertheless, his varied career and organizational talents made him an ideal theater commander. Kesselring had begun his military career in the Bavarian artillery, being elevated to the general staff in the winter of 1917 as a result of his demonstrated talent. He remained in the Reichswehr in the 1930s, until 1933 when he was ordered to become chief administrator of the Air Ministry in civilian mufti. His primary responsibility was the creation of the infrastructure of the new Luftwaffe, and this attracted the favorable attention of the Luftwaffe head, Hermann Göring. By the time war broke out, he had returned to uniform as commander of Luftflotte 1, the tactical close-support bomber and Stuka force that played such a prominent role in the 1939 campaign against Poland and later as commander of Luftflotte 2 during the 1940 campaign against France. Kesselring was appointed to OB-Süd in December 1941 and given the politically challenging task of co-ordinating the German war effort in North Africa with Mussolini and the Comando Supremo. His political charms led to his nickname "Smiling Albert". Kesselring carried out his tasks with considerable skill, managing to keep the Italians mollified while keeping some of the more rambunctious German commanders such as Erwin Rommel in check. In spite of his lack of experience in divisional or corps commands, he proved to be an astute and effective operational leader and certainly one of Germany's most talented strategic commanders during the war.

The two main army formations in Italy in early 1944 were the 10th Army commanded by Generaloberst Heinrich Gottfried von Vietinghoff-Scheel, and the 14th Army under Generaloberst Eberhard von Mackensen. Vietinghoff won the Iron Cross as a young Prussian infantry officer of the Guards in World War I. At the beginning of World War I, he was commander of the 5th Panzer Division in Poland in 1939, and his talents as a field commander led to his steady rise, commanding the 13th Army Corps in France in 1940, the 46th Panzer Corps in Russia in 1941, and the 9th Army in Russia in September 1942. He was promoted to Colonel General in September 1943 and posted to Italy on 15 August 1943. When Kesselring left Italy in October 1944, Vietinghoff took his place as the OB-Südwest.

Mackensen was another talented Prussian officer, but with a career oriented towards staff positions rather than field commands. He was the son of the legendary Generalfeldmarschall August von Mackensen of World War I fame, and the brother of Hans Georg von Mackensen, the German ambassador to Italy during the war. He won the Iron Cross in World War I as a young officer, served as the chief of staff of the 14th Army at the outbreak of the war in 1939, and chief of staff of the 12th Army from November 1939 to January 1942 when he was assigned to command the 3rd Panzer Corps on the Eastern Front. His success in this role led to his promotion to lead the 1st Panzer Army during the Stalingrad campaign in November 1942 where he remained through the summer 1943 battles, finally being transferred to the 14th Army command in Italy in November 1943. Mackensen was sacked by Kesselring on 5 June 1944, following the fall of Rome, for failing to carry out orders.

The two Allied commanders most involved in the planning of Operation *Shingle* were the 15th Army Group commander, General Sir Harold R.L.G. Alexander, and the Fifth Army commander, MajGen Mark W. Clark, seen here on 30 April 1944 with Clark being decorated with the Order of the British Empire. (NARA)

ALLIED COMMANDERS

No Allied commander played a greater role in promoting Operation *Shingle* than Prime Minister Winston Churchill. The landing plans had largely fallen out of favor until mid-December 1943 when Churchill latched upon it as a means to reinvigorate the Italian campaign and speed along the liberation of Rome. Churchill's considerable political influence was the major reason why the operation proceeded in spite of the misgivings of the tactical commanders.

When Dwight Eisenhower left the Mediterranean theater in late 1943 to take over Operation *Overlord* in Britain, he was replaced by Field Marshal Henry Maitland Wilson. However, the most influential theater commander in Italy was Gen Sir Harold Alexander, who led the 15th Army Group. Alexander had been appointed to command of the 18th Army Group in February 1943 during the concluding phase of the North African campaign in Tunisia. Alexander was highly regarded by Churchill who frequently turned to him for advice, and by Eisenhower who saw in him a commander like himself who could manage the fractious and egotistical British and American generals under his command. "Alex" was enormously popular amongst the troops for his unpretentious courage and frequent visits to the front, and his optimism

MajGen John P. Lucas, commander of VI Corps during Operation *Shingle*.

MajGen Lucian K. Truscott Jr., commander of the US Army 3rd Division at the time of the Anzio landing, and subsequently VI Corps commander after Lucas' relief. (NARA)

Col William O. Darby commanded the ill-fated US Ranger force at Anzio. (MHI)

helped buoy the spirits of many of his divisional commanders during the dismal Italian campaign. Montgomery considered him a lightweight in tactical skills, and his principal American subordinate, Mark Clark, was always suspicious that he planned to steal the limelight from himself, the Fifth Army, and the US effort in general. If military historians have reached any consensus on Alexander, it has been that his restrained style of leadership depended more upon persuasion than clear and direct orders, so leaving many critical decisions in the hands of headstrong subordinate commanders who did not agree with his viewpoint. This would be the case in Alexander's relationship with Clark, who was sometimes able to evade Alexander's intentions.

Alexander's two principal subordinate commanders in Italy were Gen Bernard Montgomery, who commanded the British Eighth Army on the eastern, Adriatic side of Italy and LtGen Mark Clark, who commanded the US Fifth Army on the western side of Italy. As a result, Clark was the principal tactical commander of the Anzio operation. Clark graduated from West Point in 1917 and was wounded on his first day of combat in France in 1918. His postings in the interwar years were primarily in staff positions. He was a hard-driving, enormously ambitious officer, noted for his personal courage. Clark was equally well known for his vanity, self-confidence and self-promotion. In October 1942, he landed from a US submarine off the coast of French North Africa to conduct discussions with senior French officials in hopes of averting French resistance to the planned Operation *Torch* landings in Morocco and Algeria. Clark took command of the Fifth Army prior to the landings at Salerno in September 1943. Reactions to his leadership at Salerno were mixed. He was decorated with the Distinguished Service Cross for conspicuous bravery for his frontline command style, but many observers blamed his decisions for the nearly disastrous outcome of the landings. Clark was quick to blame others for the problems, especially British officers such as Conigham and Tedder who led the Allied air forces in the Mediterranean theater. In contrast to Eisenhower who insisted on maintaining proper if not friendly relations with the British, Clark was openly contemptuous of British commanders and vocal about his disdain for British imperial interests in the Mediterranean. His relations with Alexander were polite and proper in public, but argumentative and difficult in private to the point that aides recommended more than once that he be relieved of command.

The principal Allied tactical commander at Anzio was the VI Corps commander, MajGen John P. Lucas. Older than Clark, a member of the 1911 West Point class, Lucas had been severely wounded in 1918 in France. He commanded the 3rd Infantry Division at the beginning of the war, and in 1942–43 was the III Corps commander in the United States. He was highly regarded by both the chief of staff of the army, George Marshall, and by Eisenhower and served as Ike's liaison officer to Patton's Seventh Army during the Sicily operations. Lucas took command of the VI Corps following the relief of its previous commander, Ernest Dawley in the wake of the problems during the Salerno operations. Lucas led the VI Corps during the difficult autumn and winter 1943 fighting including the bloody fighting for the Rapido river. Lucas was highly regarded by senior US commanders and indeed Eisenhower had considered him at one point as a possible Fifth Army commander. But the bloody autumn fighting in Italy left him exhausted and depressed. He was skeptical about the prospects for Operation *Shingle* from the outset, and his known aversion to the plan led to his exclusion at key conferences involved in planning the operation, including Churchill's January meeting in Marrakesh. In his diary he noted that, "This whole affair had a strong odor of Gallipoli and apparently the same amateur was still on the coaches bench," a reference to Churchill and the disastrous landings he had advocated on the Turkish coast in World War I. Lucas made no secret of his forebodings about the operation, which led some officers to urge him to resign, and others to recommend that Alexander find another commander. Alexander refused, arguing that it would be a mistake to do so with the operation so near.

THE OPPOSING ARMIES

GERMAN FORCES

The two principal German formations in Italy in January 1944 were the 10th and 14th Armies, under the command of Army Group C. Both commands were similar in size, but had significantly different missions. The 10th Army was assigned the combat role of holding the Gustav line from Gaeta on the western shore to the Ortona sector on the Adriatic coast, with the Apennine mountains stretching in the middle. The 14th Army was assigned the garrison role further north.

The 10th Army consisted of the 14th Corps on the Cassino front and the 76th Panzer Corps on the Adriatic front, with a strength typically of about 10 divisions. The 10th Army bore the brunt of the fighting and its divisional components varied from week to week as units were taken off the line for rest and recuperation in central Italy, and their places taken by refreshed divisions. The boundary line with the 14th Army was positioned slightly above Rome, but in fact the defense of the Rome area was allotted to the 11th Luftwaffe Corps, directly under Army Group C control. In mid January 1944, plans were under way to shift the 90th Panzergrenadier Division from the Adriatic side towards Rome and to relieve the battered 29th Panzergrenadier Division near Cassino. When the US Fifth Army launched its attack along the Garigliano river on 18 January, the defensive front nearly broke open, and forced Kesselring to commit both the 29th and the 90th Panzergrenadier Divisions to the Garigliano front under the command of the 1st Fallschirmjäger Corps. While this succeeded in stopping the US attack, it left the area south of Rome near Anzio denuded of major troop concentrations.

The Luftwaffe had a significant presence in the Anzio operation with two of its divisions deployed there. This young Fallschirmjäger wears the Luftwaffe eagle insignia and paratrooper camouflage smock. He is carrying the distinctive Fallschirmjäger helmet under his left arm.

The 14th Army consisted of the 87th Army Corps and the 51st Mountain Corps, and usually had a strength of about 9 divisions. The role of the 14th Army was significantly different from the 10th Army. Its only combat mission was to conduct anti-partisan operations in northern Italy, a mission that increased in intensity in the final year of the war due to the rise of the Italian partisan movement. However, the 14th Army had several other significant missions. Its divisions were seldom at combat strength, but rather were divisions that had been withdrawn from the Russian front for reconstruction, divisions from the 10th Army being refreshed prior to return to combat, or new divisions being

The significant number of German light infantry formations in Italy led to the extensive use of specialized equipment like this Püppchen 88mm anti-tank rocket launcher captured in the Cisterna area in May 1944. (NARA)

The 150mm Nebelwerfer multiple rocket launcher was dubbed the "Screamin' Meemie" due to the frightening sound of its rockets. A rocket is seen here alongside the launcher as well as its transport tube. (NARA)

created in Italy. The 14th Army had several static defense missions including coastal defense of northern Italy, and the creation of defensive lines in central and northern Italy such as the Gothic Line in the event that the Allies broke through the Gustav line. The army also supervised two operational zones, GenLt Kubler's Adriatic Coastal Region in today's Slovenia, and GenLt Witthoft's Alpine Approaches Region in the Venice–Ancona area on the Adriatic defending the passes into southern Germany through the Alps.

The German defenses near Anzio in mid-January were very modest. The defense sector from the mouth of the Tiber river, past Anzio to the mouth of the Astura river, 40 miles (65 km) in length, was covered by only two engineer companies of the new 4th Fallschirmjäger Division, plus one engineer company and one panzergrenadier battalion of the 29th Panzergrenadier Division. Coastal defense batteries totaled 41 guns of various calibers, the largest of which was a battery of six 170mm guns.

Luftwaffe strength in Italy had been weakened since the loss of Sicily and the autumn 1943 fighting. The bomber force was divided between

The standard German heavy self-propelled gun was the 150mm Hummel based on the PzKpfw IV chassis. This example was lost near Cisterna in late May 1944. (NARA)

about 50 medium bombers in Greece and Crete and 60 medium bombers in southern France. The main Luftwaffe strength in Italy was in fighters, totaling about 230 in January 1943 with about a third of this force near Rome. The fighter force was significantly debilitated in the weeks before the Anzio landing by concentrated Allied air attacks against the airbases which cratered runways, destroyed fuel and maintenance facilities and damaged a portion of the Luftwaffe air strength.

Kriegsmarine strength in the Mediterranean was modest, including a single U-boat flotilla and three S-boat flotillas, but lacked any warships the size of a destroyer. Allied naval superiority as well as intensive air attacks confined most of the German naval activity to the Adriatic.

Since the withdrawal of Italy from the Axis in September 1943 and the disarming of the Italian army, Italian units no longer played a significant role in German defensive plans. The creation of a puppet Italian republic under Mussolini along with an associated military force was under way but had no consequence during the Anzio operation.

ALLIED FORCES

The initial VI Corps landing at Anzio consisted of two divisions, the British 1st Division on the left flank northwest of Anzio, and the US 3rd Infantry Division to the southeast of Nettuno. The original plans had presumed that the landings would be conducted solely by US troops, but after Christmas, Churchill made it plain to Alexander that he "did not like that the first and most risky operation undertaken in the Mediterranean under British command should fall exclusively upon American forces."

The VI Corps commander's main concern was not the mixed composition of the force, but rather their lack of recent training in amphibious operations. Lucas insisted that the invasion be postponed to provide more training, but Churchill resisted any such changes and instead landing rehearsals were conducted on 19 January, only three days before the landings. The British landings near Salerno were adequate, but the US

There was an unusually high proportion of elite light infantry committed to the Anzio fighting on both sides. This is Staff Sgt. Cyril Krotzer of the HQ, 2nd Regiment seen here after a raid on 15 April by the 1st Special Service Force wearing the distinctive insignia of this formation.

Troops of the doomed 1st Ranger Battalion board their LCIs in Baia harbor on 16 January 1944. The Ranger flash is barely evident on their shoulder, but they wear the cloth helmet cover peculiar to Darby's Rangers. (NARA)

One of the more intriguing Allied innovations used at Anzio was the addition of a flight deck to LSTs by 3rd Division engineers. This permitted L-4 observation aircraft to fly artillery observation missions from offshore when airbases were not available in the beachhead. (NARA)

3rd Division practice landing was a fiasco. The craft were launched so far from shore that most took three or four hours to reach the beaches, and then not a single battalion managed to land at the correct time, correct location, or in proper formation. Forty DUKW amphibious trucks swamped and sank, along with 19 105mm howitzers. Admiral Frank Lowry, the commander of Task Force 81 assigned to conduct the amphibious landings at Anzio, argued that it would be impractical to conduct the landings without further training. This was dismissed out of hand due to the timetable. In the event, the landings faced few difficulties as they were largely uncontested.

Besides the two infantry divisions, the other forces earmarked for the landing included three US Ranger battalions, two British Commando battalions and a US airborne regiment. A regiment of the 45th Division and two combat commands of the 1st Armored Division were held in reserve at Naples for potential reinforcement.

Preparations for Operation *Shingle* included vigorous efforts by the Mediterranean Allied Air Forces (MAAF) to isolate the landing beaches from German reinforcements by an air campaign against the road and rail network. A general air campaign began on 2 January 1944, and intensified near Anzio on 13 January. In total some 22,850 sorties were flown by the MAAF in the twenty days before the landings, but the consensus by the army afterward was that it had failed to accomplish its mission. The German view was somewhat different, and the Allied air attacks certainly hastened the downward spiral of the Luftwaffe in the Italian theater. A significant contribution was the raid on 19 January by the B-24s of the 449th Bomb Group which wrecked the German airbase at Perugia, making it unserviceable for the reconnaissance aircraft there around the time of the landings, and thereby helping to ensure tactical surprise for Operation *Shingle*.

Allied Landings Forces, Operation *Shingle*, 22 January 1944

Task Force 81	**Rear Admiral Admiral Frank J. Lowry, USN**
Task Force X-Ray	**Rear Admiral Admiral Frank J. Lowry, USN**
3rd Infantry Division (US)	MajGen Lucian K. Truscott Jr.
6615th Ranger Force (Provisional)	Col. William O. Darby
504th Parachute Infantry Regiment	Col. Reuben H. Tucker
Task Force Peter	**Rear Admiral Thomas Troubridge, RN**
1st Division (British)	MajGen W.R.C. Penney
2nd Special Service Brigade	Brig. R.J.F. Tod

OPPOSING PLANS

THE ALLIED PLAN

Discussions over future plans for the Italian campaign began in late October and early November between the Supreme Allied Commander, Gen Dwight Eisenhower, and the principal theater commanders, including Gen Harold Alexander of the 15th Army Group and Gen Mark Clark of the Fifth Army. The general consensus was that an amphibious end-run around the Gustav line would be desirable if sufficient amphibious vessels could be provided. The aim of the operation at the strategic level was to facilitate the capture of Rome. The operational aim was to dislodge the German defenders in the Gustav line and force them to retreat. On 8 November 1943, Alexander outlined the aims of the operation to Clark, stating that the objective would be to direct the landings against the Alban hills south of Rome, and in combination with a renewed offensive opposite the Gustav line, force the Germans to abandon their defenses on the western side of the Apennines south of Rome.

The Fifth Army G-3 staff prepared a more detailed plan during the middle of November codenamed Operation *Shingle*, and it was approved by Clark on 25 November. The plan clarified several ambiguous elements of the earlier discussions. To begin with, *Shingle* assumed that the invasion force would be relatively small, due to the lack of shipping, about a division in size. As such, its mission would be subsidiary to the main Fifth Army

Troops from the ill-fated 3rd Ranger Battalion board their LCIs in Baia on 16 January 1944. (NARA)

In support of Operation *Shingle*, the XII Air Support Command staged numerous strikes against German lines of communication including this B-26 mission on 22 January 1944 against the Ceprano bridges. Flak can be seen bursting in the background. (MHI)

effort around Cassino. The plan depended on the advance of the Fifth Army to the line of Capistrello–Ferentino–Priverno which was about 40 miles southeast of Rome. Alexander's instructions had suggested that the Alban hills would be the main tactical objective of the landing force, but given its small size, this mission was transferred to the advancing Fifth Army. The presumption was that the *Shingle* force would link up with the main body of the Fifth Army no later than one week after the landings.

Discrepancies between the Alexander instructions and the *Shingle* plan were not immediately ironed out since the poor winter weather led to a stagnation of the Allied front around Cassino, undermining the *Shingle* concept. On 10 December, Clark revived the plan in a modified way. He proposed that *Shingle* could go ahead even without the Fifth Army in reach of the Alban hills if the *Shingle* force was strengthened and if assurances could be obtained from the Allied naval commanders that the landing area could be supported from the sea. The new version of *Shingle* presumed that the beachhead would be separated from the Fifth Army for more than a week, but that the presence of a substantial Allied force in the enemy rear would facilitate the advance of the Fifth Army on the way to Rome. This was not a convincing argument to the senior Allied commanders, and *Shingle* was canceled by Clark on 18 December ostensibly due to a lack of landing craft but also due to the failure of the Fifth Army to advance as expected past Cassino and into the Liri valley.

Churchill was extremely unhappy about the lack of progress in Italy, and called a meeting of senior Allied commanders in Tunis for Christmas day. Churchill saw *Shingle* as the last, best hope to retrieve the faltering Italian campaign. Churchill wrote Clark before the landings that "I am deeply conscious of the importance of the battle, without which the campaign will be regarded as having petered out ingloriously."

There was little enthusiasm from the military due to the obvious problems with the plan, and Eisenhower disputed Churchill's argument that a landing would prompt the Germans to withdraw from southern and central Italy. The theater intelligence officer, Gen Strong, stated his clear opposition to the plan, arguing that the Germans in the theater were too strong. When the senior Royal Navy commander in the Mediterranean, Admiral John Cunningham, warned Churchill that the operation was fraught with great risk, Churchill dismissed his concerns: "Of course there is risk, but without risk there is no honour, no glory, no adventure!"

Alexander eventually deferred to Churchill's judgment, and in the end the military commanders were badgered into accepting Churchill's wishes. If there was any military commander sympathetic to Churchill's intent, it was Clark, who shared his dream of the glory of capturing Rome. Churchill personally intervened with Roosevelt to ensure that the LSTs needed for the operation remained available in the Mediterranean through February, though Roosevelt reiterated Marshall's insistence that "*Overlord* remains the paramount operation" and that other of Churchill's pet projects such as a proposed landing on Rhodes, be sidetracked. In the event, a planned operation against the Andaman islands in the Pacific was canceled, freeing up landing ships that were subsequently used to land the British components of VI Corps at Anzio.

A remaining issue was the exact location of the landing. On the one hand, a landing in the Terracina area would place the beachhead closer to the Cassino front, immediately threatening German lines of communication, and thereby making it more likely that the Germans would withdraw from the Gustav line. The main drawback of this option was that it did not sufficiently support the strategic aim of the operation, namely the capture of Rome. A landing closer to Rome was preferred, near Anzio. The main drawback to the Anzio location was the question of whether a landing so distant from the Gustav line near Cassino would actually force a German withdrawal. The theater G-2, Gen Kenneth Strong, was pessimistic. The initial plans assumed that the Fifth Army would be able to break through at Cassino and advance on Anzio within a week, an assessment later extended to a month. In view of past German performance, Strong was skeptical that the Fifth Army would be able to break through the Gustav line, even when reinforced by the Eighth Army. Furthermore, Strong doubted the premise that the Anzio landing would force the Germans to choose between defending Rome or maintaining the defenses at Cassino. The 14th Army in Northern Italy, while not possessing first-rate units, still represented a ready reserve that had not been fully exhausted. He also questioned the notion that the Anzio landing would force a German withdrawal from the Gustav line, as Anzio was so far from Cassino that a landing there posed no immediate threat to the main lines of communication. The 15th Army Group G-2 was more optimistic, judging that the Germans had about two divisions in the Rome area and that the weather and Allied air interdiction would limit their ability to influence the bridgehead. The Fifth Army G-2 took a pessimistic attitude similar to that of Gen Strong, acknowledging the short-term threat of two division-equivalents around Rome, but also presuming that the Germans would be obliged to strip units from other areas and so probably be able to muster four divisions against the bridgehead within two weeks of the

LCI (Landing Craft, Infantry) board troops of the 504th Parachute Infantry Regiment at Pozzuoli in the harbors around Naples on 21 January 1944. A shortage of amphibious assault transport limited the size of the invading force to two divisions. (NARA)

landing. Some Allied commanders, while skeptical over whether Anzio would live up to Churchill's grand vision, felt that Operation *Shingle* would force the Germans to strip units from elsewhere in the theater, which would aid an Allied advance even if in other sectors.

The Fifth Army assessment of likely German reactions was strongly influenced by the experiences at Salerno several months before. Allied planners had underestimated the pace and scope of German reactions to the Salerno landing on 9 September 1943. As a result, the landings narrowly avoided being thrown back into the sea in a week of ferocious fighting. This had two consequences for the *Shingle* planning. It forced a continual increase in the size of the landing force. In addition, the memories of near disaster at Salerno inclined the senior Allied commanders to favor caution over boldness in executing the short-term objectives of the landing. This would create one of the primary controversies about the operation. Should the immediate objective of the landing force be to secure the beachhead to prepare for a probable German counter attack comparable to that encountered at Salerno? Or should the invasion force take a bolder approach to move out immediately and seize the Alban hills?

Alexander's intentions for the operation included an eventual seizure of the Alban hills as a means to threaten the German lifeline to the Cassino front, Highway 6, which ran along their eastern side. Clark, on the other hand, did not believe that the Alban hills would be a feasible objective in the short term with only two divisions ashore due to the distance from Anzio, so that when Lucas received his instructions on 12 January, the mission was stated to be, "seize and secure the beachhead and advance on Colli Laziali" (the Alban hills). In view of the uncertainties of the German response, these ambiguous instructions were intended to provide some degree of flexibility for Lucas.

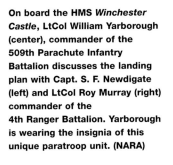

On board the HMS *Winchester Castle*, LtCol William Yarborough (center), commander of the 509th Parachute Infantry Battalion discusses the landing plan with Capt. S. F. Newdigate (left) and LtCol Roy Murray (right) commander of the 4th Ranger Battalion. Yarborough is wearing the insignia of this unique paratroop unit. (NARA)

With memories of the near disaster at Salerno still fresh in the minds of the Allied commanders, a cautious response should have been expected. Other events reinforced this perception. The plan originally included an air-drop of the 504th Parachute Infantry Regiment on the Anzio–Via Anziate about ten miles to the north of Anzio. This would have provided an incentive to the commander to push the bridgehead further out and much faster to ensure a link-up. In the event, it was dropped prior to the landings ostensibly because the commanders in the British sector near where the paratroopers would be operating complained that they might be mistaken for Germans and brought under friendly fire. In fact, it was viewed as too risky. The British 1st Division commander, Gen Penney, wrote after the war that VI Corps could have pushed boldly out of the beachhead but "we would have had one night in Rome and 18 months in prisoner of war camps."

In the event, the Anzio plan was a confused mess, flawed by Churchill's romantic longings for martial glory, by wishful thinking and by a willful refusal to consider the likely German response. It was not until after the war that Churchill conceded that "Anzio was my worst moment of the war. I had the most to do with it." It was a mission for an entire army, not a single corps, and without such resources it was ill-fated from the start. Anzio was a risky gamble executed by armies and commanders averse to risk.

GERMAN PLANS

In mid-January, the head of the German Abwehr intelligence agency, Admiral Wilhelm Canaris, stated in an assessment of the Italian theater that "there is not the slightest sign that a new landing would be undertaken in the near future." This wildly incorrect assessment was based in part on the assumption that the Allied navies could not conduct another amphibious landing so soon after Salerno, but it was also due to the success of the Allied air forces in blinding the Luftwaffe by attacks against reconnaissance squadron air bases in the days leading up to the operation. German intelligence assessments at this point of the war were poor and declining in quality.

Even if misled by intelligence assessments about the timing of the Anzio operation, Kesselring and the senior German commanders had long anticipated the strong possibility of an Allied landing that might be used to cut off the 10th Army. The Allies themselves encouraged such considerations by staging deception operations, creating illusory landing plans against many points on the Italian coast in the hope of tying down German units in worthless coastal defense missions. At the end of December 1943, the German high command completed a contingency plan called Marder 1 and issued a set of instructions to OB-West (France), OB-Südost (the Balkans) and OB-Sudwest (Italy) outlining their responsibilities for dispatching reinforcements in the event of various Allied amphibious landings in Italy. Five main contingencies were considered: Case Richard (Rome area); Ludwig (Livorno); Gustav (Genoa); Viktor (Adriatic coast); and Ida (Istria/Trieste). The reinforcements for the Rome sector planned under Case Richard included a Panzer or Panzergrenadier division, a Panzer reconnaissance battalion

Nettuno and Anzio harbors were protected by numerous bunkers and gun positions, but few of these were manned when the Allies landed on 22 January 1944. This camouflaged bunker is in Nettuno harbor. (NARA)

and an artillery battalion from the 10th Army; a paratroop division and assault gun battalion from the 11th Luftwaffe Corps; and an infantry division, two reinforced infantry divisions and a Panzergrenadier division from the 14th Army.

Allied planners were unaware of the Marder/Case Richard plans and underestimated the German ability to reinforce the Rome area quickly. Operation *Shingle* presumed that, within two weeks of the landings, the Germans would only be able to muster about 60,000 troops opposite the beachhead. In reality, the Germans managed to transfer nearly a third more troops, over 90,000, to the Anzio area in this time-frame. The Allied plans overestimated the impact of Allied air power in limiting the transfers and underestimated the capability of the Wehrmacht to shift forces from other theaters.

In early January, there were plans to conduct another round of divisional transfers to permit battered units on the Cassino front to rebuild. So, for example, the 29th Panzergrenadier Division was scheduled to be removed from the front lines and shifted to the Rome area where it would replace the 3rd Panzergrenadier Division while rebuilding. This proved to be difficult to accomplish due to the continued fighting along the front, and when the US Fifth Army launched its Garagliano–Rapido offensive on 18 January, the 3rd Panzergrenadier Division was rushed from the Rome area when the right flank of the 10th Army was threatened. As a result, German reserves in the Rome–Anzio area were more depleted than usual when the Allies landed.

GEOGRAPHIC FACTORS

The landing areas consisted of shallow beaches near the two nearby resort towns of Anzio and Nettuno. The area behind the beaches was a coastal plain, bordering on the Pontine marshes to the southeast. The coastal area was a typical tidal area, and poorly drained until Mussolini's Fascist administration started a public works effort in the 1930s to reclaim the land for farming and reduce the risks of malaria and other

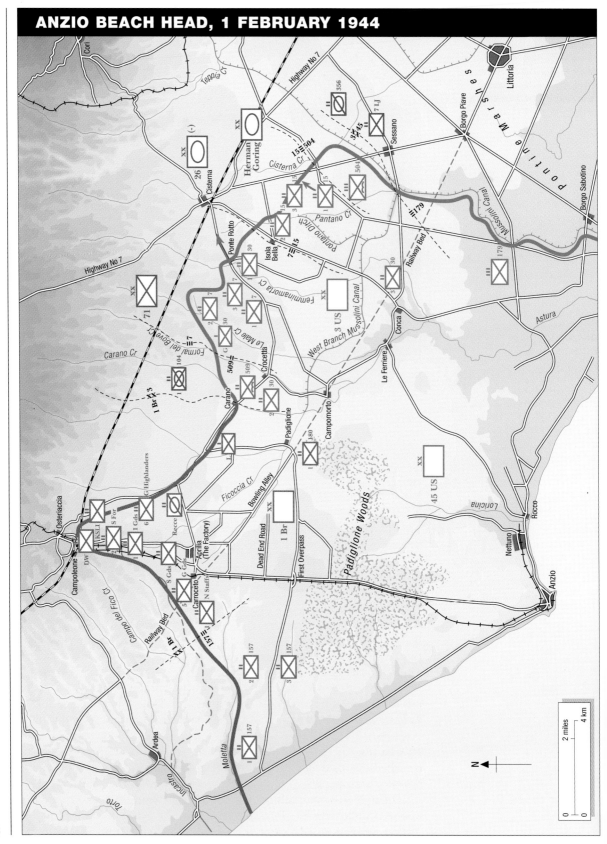

German naval operations against the Anzio beachhead included torpedo-boat attacks by S-boats like these of the 1st Schnellboot Division, seen in an Italian port in 1945 after the capitulation. (MHI)

One of the innovations deployed against Anzio were these small, Goliath demolition vehicles. They were packed with high explosives and remotely controlled by wire against defensive positions. They were not notably successful and this example was captured by the 1st SSF in April 1944. (NARA)

diseases which had plagued the area for centuries. This program created the Mussolini canal at the southeastern side of the beachhead, as well as a series of irrigation gullies, locally called *fosso*, which crisscrossed the fields. Several sturdy villages had been created in the 1930s as part of the public works effort, the most consequential of which for the fighting at Anzio was Aprilia. It had been constructed as a model Fascist farming community with its own cinema, shops, chapel, homes, and winery, all built in a particularly durable fashion. Aprilia was dubbed "The Factory" by Allied troops due to a prominent bell tower which reminded them of a factory smokestack.

The area was generally flat with little major vegetation except for the wooded Bosco di Padiglione. The main road was the Via Anziate from Anzio to Albano which connected to Highway 7 beyond the Campoleone station, the main coastal road to Rome. The other major road ran from Nettuno to Cisterna, also joining Highway 7. There was also a network of railroads as well as a disused rail bed running through the area that took on undue importance due to the featureless nature of much of the rest of the terrain. Although not immediately evident to either the Allied planners or to the German defenders, the terrain around Anzio was ill-suited to combat. The ground conditions, already damp due to the low water table, turned to mud during the rainy winter months. Trenches soon became full of water and mud, sometimes only a foot below the surface. These conditions also made it difficult to operate tanks and tracked vehicles off the roads since they quickly became trapped in the mud.

Beyond the beachhead were the Alban hills, also known as the Colli Laziali. This hill mass arose abruptly from the coastal plains, and was in fact the remains of two extinct volcanoes, with two mountain lakes in the craters. The Alban hills at their highest point rose to 3,100 feet (950 meters), providing an ideal vantage to observe the entire surrounding countryside including the beachhead area. The military significance of the Alban hills was not so much their terrain but the fact that they sat astride the two main coastal roads leading to Rome, both Highways 6 and 7.

THE CAMPAIGN

OPERATION *SHINGLE*

The invasion fleet departed Naples on 21 January and included four Liberty transport ships, eight LSIs, 84 LSTs, 96 LCIs and 50 LCTs, supported by five cruisers, 24 destroyers and a host of support vessels. The fleet anchored off Anzio in the early morning hours of 22 January 1944, and at 0150 hours a pair of British landing craft fitted with rockets fired an initial barrage against the landing beaches with no reply from the shore. The first assault wave headed to shore at 0200 hours, fully expecting stiff resistance. To the great surprise and relief of the Allied commanders, there was virtually no resistance at all. A few shore batteries attempted to interfere with the landings before dawn, but were quickly silenced by naval gunfire. There were also a small number of anti-aircraft guns in the area which fired on Allied aircraft. The Luftwaffe attempted to stage several raids against the invasion force, and six Bf-109 fighters managed to break through the Allied air cover early in the morning and make a fast run over the beaches, setting fire to a few trucks at Beach Red. Later in the morning, some FW-190 fighters staged a raid against the fleet, sinking an LCI with a bomb. In total, the Luftwaffe launched about 50 fighter sorties against the beachhead during daylight hours, losing seven fighters while downing three Allied fighters.

The US 3rd Infantry Division landed south of Anzio along with the supporting 751st Tank Battalion, and by mid-morning pushed inland three miles to set up a defensive perimeter. The British 1st Division landed north of Anzio and by late morning had pushed out about two miles from the beaches while the Commandos established a blocking

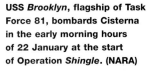

USS *Brooklyn*, flagship of Task Force 81, bombards Cisterna in the early morning hours of 22 January at the start of Operation *Shingle*. (NARA)

OPERATION SHINGLE, 22 JANUARY 1944

Between 0500 hours and 2400 hours, Task Force 81, Task Force X-Ray and Task Force Peter land on their designated beaches.

Note: Gridlines are shown at intervals of 2 Kilometers

xx
1
PENNEY

Task Force Peter

3
RED
18
4
YELLOW
22
5
GREEN
26

17

19

23

24

25

2

14

15

13

ANZIO

10

NETT

YELLOW

6

Task Force 81

1

III
6115 Rn
DARBY

TASK FORCES

Task Force 81
2 command ships
4 Liberty ships

Task Force X-Ray
1 HQ Ship
1 Cruiser
8 Destroyers
2 Destroyer Escorts
6 Mine Sweepers
12 Submarine Chasers (173')
20 Submarine Chasers (110')
18 Motor Mine Sweepers
6 Repair Ships
267 Landing Vessels
    Corps (21 LST, 17 LSI, 1 AGC)
    3rd Division (2 LSI, 37 LCT, 29 LST,
    43 LCI, 26 LCA, 60 LCVP)
    Ranger Force (3 LSI, 1 LST, 2 LCT,
    25 LCA)

Task Force Peter
1 HQ Ship
4 Cruisers
8 Fleet Destroyers
6 Hunt Destroyers
2 Anti-aircraft Ships
2 Gunboats (Dutch)
11 Fleet Mine Sweepers
6 Small Mine Sweepers
4 LCG (Landing Craft, Gun)
4 LCF (Landing Craft, Flak)
4 LCT(R) (Landing Craft Tank (Rocket))
141 Landing Vessels
    1 Division (1 AGC, 3 LSI, 30 LST, 18
    LCT, 24 LCI, 41 LCA, 24 LCVP)

▼ EVENTS

1. 0005 HOURS: Task Force 81 dropped anchor off Cape Anzio.

2. 0150 HOURS: two British LCT (R) each fire **798 5-inch rockets against landing beaches**

3. 0200 HOURS: British 2 Infantry Brigade landings on Beach Red, advances to edge of Padiglione woods by early morning.

4. 0200 HOURS: British 24 Guards Brigade begins landing in center of Peter Beach on Beach Yellow, establishes defenses in Padiglione woods by mid-morning.

5. 0200 HOURS: British 2 Special Service Brigade lands on Beach Green and pushes out to the south-east edge of the Padiglione woods.

6. 0200 HOURS: 6615th Ranger Force lands on Beach Yellow between Anzio and Nettuno. Its three battalions and the attached 509th Parachute Infantry Battalion establish a perimeter about a mile from Anzio-Nettuno in the morning.

xx
3
TRUSCOTT

7. 0200 HOURS: 7th Infantry lands on Beach Red and its three battalions establish western perimeter of X-Ray beach, with the 1/7th Infantry pushing out to link up with the British Commandos near the Padiglione woods.

8. 0200 HOURS: 30th Infantry lands on Beach Red in the center of X-Ray Beach, and during the day push up the road towards Le Ferriere.

9. 0200 HOURS: 15th Infantry lands on Beach Green and its three battalions establish the landing zone's eastern perimeter.

10. 2400 HOURS: Task Force 81 has landed 36,000 troops and 3,200 vehicles by the end of the day.

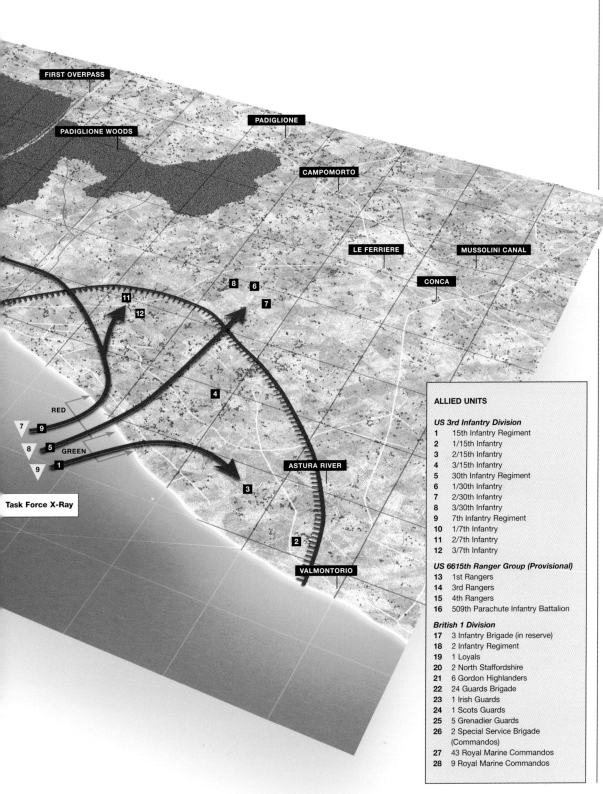

FIRST OVERPASS

PADIGLIONE

PADIGLIONE WOODS

CAMPOMORTO

LE FERRIERE

MUSSOLINI CANAL

CONCA

8 6

7

11

12

4

RED

7 9

8 5 GREEN

9 1

ASTURA RIVER

3

2

Task Force X-Ray

VALMONTORIO

ALLIED UNITS

US 3rd Infantry Division
1 15th Infantry Regiment
2 1/15th Infantry
3 2/15th Infantry
4 3/15th Infantry
5 30th Infantry Regiment
6 1/30th Infantry
7 2/30th Infantry
8 3/30th Infantry
9 7th Infantry Regiment
10 1/7th Infantry
11 2/7th Infantry
12 3/7th Infantry

US 6615th Ranger Group (Provisional)
13 1st Rangers
14 3rd Rangers
15 4th Rangers
16 509th Parachute Infantry Battalion

British 1 Division
17 3 Infantry Brigade (in reserve)
18 2 Infantry Regiment
19 1 Loyals
20 2 North Staffordshire
21 6 Gordon Highlanders
22 24 Guards Brigade
23 1 Irish Guards
24 1 Scots Guards
25 5 Grenadier Guards
26 2 Special Service Brigade
   (Commandos)
27 43 Royal Marine Commandos
28 9 Royal Marine Commandos

A US LST comes under attack by Luftwaffe bombers during landings at Anzio on 22 January 1944. (NARA)

Troops of the US 3rd Division come ashore at X-Ray beach on 22 January from LCIs, while a craft hit by a Luftwaffe bombing raid burns in the background. (MHI)

position on the road leading to Albano. The port of Anzio was seized by Darby's three Ranger battalions, and the 509th Parachute Infantry Battalion occupied the neighboring town of Nettuno, later reinforced by the 504th Parachute Infantry Regiment. Mines proved to be the only major threat. One of the few problems to crop up during the landings was the gradient of the beach in the British sector which was too shallow for efficient unloading. So Lucas instructed the navy to switch landing British forces to Anzio itself where the beaches were more suitable. Total Allied casualties on the first day were 13 killed, 97 wounded and 44 missing while 227 enemy troops were captured. By the end of the day VI Corps had landed 36,000 men, 3,200 vehicles and about a week of supplies in a textbook operation. Lucas' fears about the lack of adequate amphibious training proved unwarranted due to the lack of German forces near the beaches.

The German command in Italy, although wary of an amphibious operation such as Operation *Shingle,* did not expect such a landing while the offensive was taking place along the Garigliano river. The Allied air

US infantry comes ashore at
X-Ray Beach from an LCI
on 22 January 1944. (NARA)

US infantry comes ashore at X-Ray Beach from an LCI on 22 January 1944. (NARA)

attacks of the preceding two weeks were interpreted as being in support of the planned operations near Cassino, not a pre-invasion bombardment. As a result, *Shingle* achieved complete tactical surprise.

The first news of the landings arrived at Army Group C headquarters around 0500 hours and Kesselring immediately called the 4th Fallschirmjäger Division, forming near Rome, and the replacement formations of the Panzer Division Hermann Göring near Rome, and instructed them to rush all available troops to block the roads leading into Rome and from Anzio to the Alban hills. To confuse matters, the Allied navies had also conducted a pre-dawn bombardment of the coastal town of Civitavecchia, north of Anzio, along with fake landing maneuvers. This concerned Kesselring enough that he ordered the harbor there demolished, though within a short time it became evident that the attack there was a diversion. Once it was clear that the main landing was occurring at Anzio, Army Group C sent a report around 0600 hours to the Wehrmacht high command (OKW) in Berlin, describing what was known about the landings, and requesting that Case Richard be activated. As a result, the OKW alerted a significant number of units as detailed on the accompanying chart, though it took time to actually transport these units to the front.

Case Richard Transfers to Anzio Front, 22 – 23 January 1944

OB-West
715th Motorized Infantry Division
Artillery Battalion 998
1/Panzer Regiment 4
Panzer Abt. 301

OB-Südest
114th Light Jäger Division
Two artillery battalions

OB-Südwest
14th Army
92nd Infantry Division

65th Infantry Division (-one regiment)
362nd Infantry Division (-one regiment)
16th SS Pz.Grenadier Division

10th Army
Kampfgruppe, H. Goring Panzer Division (3 pz.gren. bn.; 1 artillery bn.)
Kampfgruppe, 15th Panzer Division (1 pz.gren. regt.; 2 arty. Bn.)
Regiment Brandenburg (-)
Nebelwerfer Regiment 56
Engineer Battalion 60

Replacement Army-Germany
HQ, 75th Corps
Infantry Lehr Regiment
Artillery Lehr Regiment
s.Pz. Abt. 508 (Tiger tanks)
Grenadier Regiment 1026
Grenadier Regiment 1027
Three battalions of security troops
Two Ost Battalion (Russian volunteers)
Six engineer-construction battalions

Kesselring now faced the dilemma of how to immediately create a defensive belt around Anzio until all these miscellaneous units arrived in the Rome area. Around 0830, he called Vietinghoff at 10th Army headquarters and ordered him to strip a corps headquarters and as many troops as he could spare and send them to the Anzio area. Vietinghoff assigned the mission to the 1st Fallschirmjäger Corps, with its component units to include units currently in reserve including the 3rd Panzergrenadier Division (minus one regiment), 71st Infantry Division, and elements of the Panzer Division Hermann Göring. These units could move that day. He also instructed 26th Panzer Division and the 1st Fallschirmjäger Division to send what units they could.

By the end of the day, Kesselring was relieved to note that the Allies seemed to be in no big rush to push out from the beachhead, and there seemed to be no indications that a major attack was being prepared. Both Vietinghoff and Gen Frido Senger und Etterlin of the 14th Panzer Corps recommended a withdrawal from the Garigliano–Rapido front near Cassino to shorten the lines and free up two seasoned divisions. Kesselring decided it was worth the risk to maintain the current defensive positions on the expectation that the Allies would be slow and cautious pushing out from the beachhead. To his credit, Kesselring was not unnerved by the Allied operation, and made astute judgments about the likely Allied conduct based on his extensive experience in the theater since the North African campaign. He had come to expect cautious action on the part of the Allies, and in the case of Anzio, he was not mistaken. Kesselring's view was reinforced later when a copy of the *Shingle* plan was captured, making it clear that there was no immediate scheme to capture the Alban hills and cut Highway 6.

Had Allied VI Corps pushed out from Anzio on 23 January, they would have encountered no significant German forces. Indeed, a reconnaissance jeep patrol from the US 3rd Division reached the outskirts of Rome on the morning of 22 January without encountering any opposition. The first significant encounters between the landing force and German defenses occurred the night of 22 January when a unit from Panzer Division

Motorized elements of the US 3rd Division come ashore on X-Ray beach on 22 January 1944 with a LST evident in the background. (NARA)

Hermann Göring seized some of the bridges over the Mussolini canal on the right flank of the beachhead. The following evening, the US 3rd Division struck back with a regimental counter attack, recapturing the bridges, and eventually demolishing them to prevent their future use.

Both Alexander and Clark visited the beachhead on 22 January and were pleased at the progress. Prior to returning to Naples, Clark warned Lucas "Don't stick your neck out Johnny. I did at Salerno, and I got into trouble." Lucas' immediate attention was focused on getting the logistical infrastructure in place to support VI Corps in the beachhead. He expected that his forces would encounter strong German rear guards if they pushed much further inland, but more importantly, he was convinced that the Germans could reinforce their defenses in front of Anzio faster than he could be reinforced from the sea. Lucas learned from Clark that the attack along the Garigliano–Rapido front had gone sour after some initial successes due to Kesselring's rapid reinforcement, which only served to reinforce his decision to hold tight. Lucas later explained his decision: "Had I been able to rush to the high ground around Albano and Velletri immediately upon landing, nothing would have been accomplished except to weaken my force by that amount of troops sent, because being completely beyond supporting distance, would have been immediately destroyed."

The relative inactivity of the Allied forces in the beachhead over the next few days has been at the heart of the Anzio controversy. Could Lucas have done more to threaten the German dispositions on the Gustav line? In view of the Salerno experience, no Allied commander seriously considered that the two divisions allotted to the landings could hold an extended perimeter that would include the Alban hills. Any short-term action would have taken the form of a raid towards the Alban hills, perhaps of regimental size. A number of such options had already been considered and rejected by *Shingle* planners including the landing of US paratroopers closer to Albano, and a raid towards Rome by Commandos. Mere Allied presence in the Alban hills was not a sufficient threat to the German lines of communication, and in fact, any such force would have needed to secure control over Highway 6 beyond the hills, to pose any real threat to the Gustav line. While Churchill may

The shallow slope of the Peter Beache proved awkward for the larger amphibious ships as seen here as a Priest 105mm self-propelled howitzer leads a motorized column of the British 1st Division ashore. As a result, subsequent British landings were directed to Anzio harbor. (NARA)

have entertained notions that such a bold move would panic the Germans and cause them to flee from the Gustav line, no experienced Allied commander who had fought against the Germans in Italy harbored any such illusions. It beggars belief that the Germans would have been intimidated by a single isolated and over extended regiment. The raiding force would have been more than twenty miles from the beachhead with an extended line of communication that was too long to be defended and vulnerable to interruption along its whole length.

A more valid criticism of the Allied actions in the first few days after the landing was the failure to establish a more defensible beachhead to encompass key road junctions such as Campoleone and Cisterna. The Anzio beachhead was relatively flat and there were few natural defensive barriers. The key towns offered one of the few defensive nodes, not only due to their control over key roads and railroads, but also because their structures offered some of the only defensive relief on the coastal plains. The *Shingle* plan had not sufficiently considered this issue since, at its heart, the beachhead was expected to be held for only a few days. Underlying the plan was the illusion that either the Fifth Army would break through the Gustav line or the German reaction would be so weak as to permit an advance on the Alban hills. The planners did not anticipate that Anzio would bog down in stalemate so did not consider the most desirable defensive perimeter.

Within a few days of the landings, the inherent flaws of the *Shingle* plan were becoming obvious to Alexander and Clark. Clark began to order more forces into the bridgehead, including the entire 45th Division instead of only a single regiment as originally planned. Two combat commands of the US 1st Armored Division were also added, since it was quickly recognized that more armored force would be needed to push out of the beachhead. On 25 January, the first regiment of the US 45th Division arrived at Anzio, to be followed by the remainder of the division as well as much of the 1st Armored Division by the end of the month. But by this time, the force ratios no longer favored the Allies.

CONTAINING THE BEACHHEAD

Since it would take days for reinforcements to arrive, Kesselring used the Luftwaffe to provide an immediate response to the Allied landings. German bombers had proved effective against the Salerno landing force, and in particular, the Do-217K bombers of Kampfgeschwader 100 armed with the new Fritz-X guided bomb. These had proven to be a significant threat to Allied warships, damaging three cruisers and the battleship HMS *Warspite* as well as sinking the Italian battleship *Roma* and damaging several other Italian capital ships when they attempted to switch sides. About the only force immediately available to Kesselring were 60 Ju-88 and He-111 medium bombers, mainly torpedo-armed, and stationed in southern France. Kesselring requested reinforcements and some of the bomber force allotted to Operation *Steinbock*, the renewed air campaign against Britain, were shifted to southern France for operations against the Anzio beaches. The reinforcements included about 60 Do-217K and He-177 bombers armed with Fritz-X guided bombs and the new Hs-293 guided anti-ship missiles.

Air attacks picked up in intensity on 23 January with a major air raid involving about 55 aircraft. Two British destroyers providing fire support off Peter Beach were hit, the HMS *Janus* was sunk by an aerial torpedo while HMS *Jervis* was hit, but not seriously damaged, by a Fritz-X guided bomb. With memories of damage inflicted by guided bombs off Salerno, the Royal Navy decided to reduce the number of gunfire support ships off Anzio as a result of the raids, sending the cruiser HMS *Penelope* back to Naples and planning to withdraw further ships until Rear Admiral Lowry angrily intervened. The daylight attacks were followed by a dusk attack by seven He-177 heavy bombers of the II/KG 40 operating from Bordeaux. The He-177 bombers dropped flares to illuminate the fleet, but the missiles failed to hit any ships. The missile-armed bombers faced a new nemesis over Anzio, radar-equipped Beaufighter night-fighters.

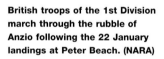

British troops of the 1st Division march through the rubble of Anzio following the 22 January landings at Peter Beach. (NARA)

ATTACKING THE FLEET, DUSK 24 JANUARY 1944
(pages 38–39)

While Kesselring raced to move reinforcements to defend the Anzio sector, he depended on the Luftwaffe to keep the Allied forces at bay. One of his trump cards was the missile armed-bomber armed with new precision guided weapons including the Fritz-X guided bomb and the Henschel Hs-293 guided missile (1). Guided weapons had proven very effective in their combat debut five months earlier off Salerno. During the Anzio campaign, the II/Kampfgeschwader 40 was based in southern France and equipped with the new He-177A Grief heavy bomber(2). The squadrons began their long-range attacks at dusk on 23 January 1944. The attacks were staged at dusk since there was less threat of Allied fighters, while at the same time, the ships of the fleet were still visible. The bombers sometimes carried out night attacks, with a portion of the bombers carrying a load of special parachute flares that would illuminate the fleet during the attack. Each bomber carried two Hs-293 missiles. The missiles were radio guided, with the operator in the nose of the bomber steering the missile remotely using a small joystick control. There was a bright flare mounted on a rear brace on the missile which helped the operator locate the missile. The missiles were fairly primitive by today's standards, and were both mechanically unreliable and difficult to steer accurately. The operator needed excellent spatial perception to determine the relationship between the missile and the target ship. Since the missile was usually released at a range of a mile or more from the ship to keep the bomber out of anti-aircraft gunfire range, the missile and target were often difficult to spot. In addition, the Allies had determined the guidance method of the missiles during the Salerno campaign and had begun to deploy radio jammers onboard some of the ships which interrupted the command signal between the bomber and the missile. This was the earliest example of electronic warfare in the missile age. However, the counter-measures were not always effective since the operator could select between several pre-determined channels. Another significant problem was the basic unreliability of the early missiles, which suffered from electrical short-circuits, engine and other mechanical problems due to the severe buffeting the missile experienced when strapped to the wing of an aircraft. Although the missile attacks against the fleet scored few hits on major warships, they had important consequences for the Anzio operation. The mere threat of the missiles convinced Allied naval commanders to send many of the cruisers back to Naples as soon as possible to avoid losses, and generally the destroyers off Anzio were sent further to sea every day in the late afternoon to make them less easy to locate and attack. The presence of the bombers helped diminish the naval firepower available to the VI Corps ashore, and naval gunfire support was much less effective at Anzio than it had been at Salerno, in no small measure due to the missile threat. (Peter Dennis)

HMS *Ulster Queen*, a converted merchantman, was illustrative of the growing sophistication of Allied amphibious operations. This ship served as a mobile fighter control center off Anzio, with secondary missions providing air defense and monitoring Luftwaffe radio channels to warn of German bomber attacks. (NARA)

An M4 medium tank of the 751st Tank Battalion departs X-Ray beach at Anzio on 22 January 1944 with the invasion fleet evident in the background. (NARA)

On the night of 23–24 January, No. 255 Squadron claimed six Ju-88, four He-177, four Do-217 and one He-111.

Allied air cover hampered Luftwaffe raids during daylight hours but around dusk on 24 January, the Luftwaffe returned in force. Over fifty fighter-bombers struck the transport area and hit the destroyer USS *Plunkett* with a 500kg bomb, and scored several near misses against the flagship USS *Brooklyn*. Three British hospital ships suffered near misses, and the *St David* was hit by an Hs-293 missile and sunk. The He-177 force from Bordeaux struck again with 11 aircraft after dark, but once more proved ineffective. Although the missile attacks claimed few victims, the threat became so great that by 26 January, Adm. Lowry ordered all cruisers and most destroyers to disperse away from the beachhead at 1600 hours each day to make them less vulnerable. On 27 January, US heavy bombers struck the main Luftwaffe bomber bases in southern France, curtailing bomber operations. In spite of these raids, on 29 January Fritz-X guided bombs struck and sank the cruiser HMS *Spartan* in the transport area as well as the cargo ship *Samuel Huntington*.

Although the air campaign against the fleet weakened the Allied naval gunfire support, Luftwaffe aircraft losses were heavy, totaling over 90 aircraft by the end of January. The situation was not helped when on 30 January, 215 US B-17 and B-24 bombers staged a series of air raids against the four main German airbases in northern Italy. Forewarned by radar of the approaching US bombers, the German squadrons tried to get aloft before the bombers struck. As the German aircraft were lifting off, they were caught near the ground by a sneak attack of P-47 Thunderbolts of the 325th Fighter Group which had swept under the cover of radar to attack at low altitude. Fourteen Bf-109 fighters and 22 bombers were shot down. By the end of the day, an estimated 140 Luftwaffe aircraft had been destroyed in the air and on the ground, substantially curtailing subsequent Luftwaffe operations over Anzio.

THE ALLIED OFFENSIVE

German army reinforcements into the Anzio sector built up faster than the Allies anticipated. Elements of five divisions were in the defensive perimeter by 25 January, though the actual strength of the German forces was closer to two full divisions. Since Vietinghoff had his hands full defending the Gustav line, Kesselring instructed Mackensen to move his 14th Army headquarters closer to the Anzio front and to take over control of its defense. The tactical headquarters was in place by the evening of 25 January and its immediate goal was to plan a counter-offensive aimed at crushing the beachhead.

The first major skirmishing in the beachhead area started on 25 January, mainly in the British sector around Aprilia on the road to the Alban hills after the British 1st Division began pushing up the road to Albano. The British thrust pushed a detachment from the 3rd Panzergrenadier Division out of the small town of Aprilia, a location that would soon become notorious as "The Factory." The fighting on 25 January was only the first of many times that these sturdy structures would change hands. In response, Pz.Gren.Rgt. 29 launched a counter-attack on 26 January supported by tanks that wrested "The Factory" from the Irish Guards and 5th Grenadiers, capturing 58 prisoners and knocking out four Sherman tanks.

By 27 January, Alexander was becoming concerned about the slow pace of operations around Anzio and Clark decided to seize Campoleone and Cisterna as an initial step towards his ultimate objective of controlling the Alban hills. Lucas was left with the impression that Clark wanted the corps to seize the towns as a means to create a viable defensive line rather than as jumping-off points for a future offensive. By the time that Alexander and Clark prodded Lucas into action, the time for easy advances had passed. The German efforts to shift troops against the beachhead were outpacing the Allied ability to move troops into the Anzio front. A week after the landing, German forces around Anzio were about 71,500 versus 61,000 Allied troops.

The first major Allied attack out of the beachhead was scheduled for the night of 29 January, a week after the landing. The 3rd Division, supported by the Rangers, was assigned to seize Cisterna while the British 1st Division was to continue up the Anzio–Via Anziate beyond "The

DUKW amphibious trucks head to the beach at Anzio on 22 January 1944. The DUKWs were the Allied secret weapon in the Mediterranean theater, able to deliver supplies to beachheads even if no port facilities were available. (NARA)

Factory" and secure Campoleone, the main road junction with the Cisterna–Rome road. By this time, Mackensen had enough forces of his own to plan an attack by three battle-groups against the bridgehead, including the newly arrived 26th Panzer Division. Although the Allies struck first, in so doing they advanced into heavily reinforced German formations preparing for their own counterattack on 1 February.

The night attack ran into heavy opposition from the beginning. The British 1st Division attack consisted of two infantry battalions supported by tanks but made little progress that night. When the attack was renewed on the afternoon of 30 January, it ran into a counter-attack force by the 3rd Panzergrenadier Division. The 1st Division fought its way into the German defenses and established a new defense line about 6km north of Aprilia. The British infantry continued the attack on 31 January, with Harmon's 1st Armored Division in support to the west of the Via Anziate. The 1st Division managed to drive a wedge between the German 65th Infantry Division and the 3rd Panzergrenadier Division, but at a dreadful cost. The Sherwood Foresters who had led the attack lost the battalion commander and every single company commander and suffered 70 percent casualties, about 560 of about 820 men. When the commander of the US 1st Armored Division visited the area near Campoleone station later in the day, he was shocked at the carnage. "I have never seen so many dead men in one place." The company he visited was down to 16 troops of the original 116, led by a corporal after all the officers had been killed or wounded. Harmon later remarked, "I think my great respect for the stubbornness and fighting ability of the British enlisted man was born that afternoon." The Campoleone station was still in German hands, and the British advance had created a narrow "Thumb" two-and-a-half miles into German lines that was ripe for counter attack.

The US 3rd Division's effort to seize Cisterna was costly but less successful. The attack began with an attempt to infiltrate two battalions of Darby's Rangers into Cisterna under the cover of darkness along the Pantano Ditch, a dry extension of the Mussolini canal that reached to within a mile of Cisterna. While the Rangers managed to reach within 800 yards of Cisterna by dawn, they had lodged themselves in the midst of the Panzer Division Hermann Göring which was preparing for the planned offensive. A wild mêlée broke out as the two Ranger battalions tried to fight their way out of the trap. Armed only with light weapons and a few bazookas, the surrounded Rangers stood little chance when assaulted by Panzers. At least two German tanks were captured but when the Rangers tried to use them to escape back to American lines, they were knocked out by other Rangers with bazookas thinking they were still in German service. In one of the skirmishes, the Germans pushed captured Rangers in front of them, trying to convince other Rangers to surrender. Of the

767 Rangers of the 1st and 3rd Battalions sent to Cisterna, only six made it back to US lines. About 450 were captured and the rest killed. One of the captured Ranger officers was later told by a German officer that German casualties had been about 400 men.

The 4th Ranger Battalion, spearheading the 3rd Division attack along the road from Isola Bella tried to break into the German defenses to relieve their fellow Rangers but were unable to do so, suffering nearly 50 per cent casualties in the process. Clark was later critical of the decision to lead the attack with the lightly armed Rangers, but Allied intelligence had seriously underestimated German strength. The survivors of the 4th Battalion were later amalgamated into another elite infantry unit sent to Anzio, the combined Canadian-American 1st Special Service Force. The attack on Cisterna continued on 31 January but with no more success. Mackensen was fully aware of the defensive value of Cisterna and had heavily reinforced the town in the day preceding the American attack. The 3rd Division now found itself defending the open ground south of the town while the Germans were firmly ensconced in the stone structures of the town itself.

The intensity of the fighting from 30 January to 1 February 1944 forced Mackensen to delay the German counter offensive scheduled for 1 February since his units were having a difficult time maintaining their positions in the face of Allied artillery and infantry attacks. Mackensen concluded that his only advantage was in artillery, which had been rushed into the beachhead area from northern Italy in anticipation of the offensive. He was especially concerned about the inadequately trained infantry from recently formed or rebuilt units who were not well suited to offensive action. As a result, on 1 February the 14th Army head-quarters instructed the troops along the main line of resistance to begin to dig in. The existing network of foxholes were to be turned into more extensive resistance points with interlocking communication trenches, minefields, and barbed wire, along with observation posts, shelters for reserves, and artillery and mortar fire support emplacements. The instructions warned that "This construction must not lower the offensive spirit of the troops. Entrenchment is a means of maintaining power for the offensive…It is the task of all commanders, especially company commanders, to fight against apathy, and to force the men to entrench themselves." The following day, a reorganization of the German defense occurred with the 65th Panzer Corps being assigned to cover the main defense line holding back the VI Corps in front of Aprilia and Cisterna. Its main components were Kampfgruppe Gräser (units from the 3rd Pz.Gren. Div. and 715th Mot. Inf. Div.); KG Raapke (reinforced 71st Infantry Division) and KG Konrad (reinforced Panzer Division Hermann Göring and 26th Panzer Division). The 1st Fallschirmjäger Corps which had been responsible for the defensive efforts had its assignment trimmed back to cover the sector from Aprilia up along the Mediterranean coast to the mouth of the Tiber river.

Mackensen visited the Cisterna front on 2 February and found that the heavy Allied bombardment had demoralized many of the inexperienced troops of Panzer Division Hermann Göring. In view of the relative abundance of artillery on the German side, he became convinced of the need to use firepower to make up for his own shortages of trained infantry, and stressed the need to his subordinate commanders to deploy forward

Shortly after landing on 22 January, troops of the British 1st Division pass a sign on the Via Anziate indicating the distance to Rome. (NARA)

observers so that the artillery could devastate any Allied attack before it reached German lines. By 5 February, 14th Army officers believed that they had an advantage of 85 artillery batteries to 59 Allied batteries, the Allies having some advantage in ammunition supply, but the Germans having an advantage in counter-battery fire due to the Allies' constricted deployment and the visibility of the Allied dispositions from the heights of the Alban hills. The arrival of the Erhart railroad artillery battery also provided the 14th Army with some long-range, heavy firepower to balance the Allied advantage in naval gunfire support. Allied naval gunfire was not as decisive at Anzio as at Salerno as the Luftwaffe threat in early February forced the navies into a more defensive posture.

Alexander visited Clark at Anzio on 1 February and expressed his displeasure at the slow pace of the advance out of the beachhead. Clark pointed out that the opposition had been much more determined than expected and he proposed that the Allies stage another landing at Civitavecchia further up the coast, further spreading German defenses and permitting an envelopment of Rome. Alexander was shocked at such a wild plan and instead both commanders agreed that the focus would be on the Anzio beachhead. In addition, Alexander acknowledged that further offensive action for the time being seemed imprudent and so Lucas was instructed to dig in and set up defenses for an anticipated German counter offensive. The 1st Special Service Force (SSF) was landed to replace the decimated Rangers and the 168th Brigade of the British 56th Division arrived on 3 February to reinforce the battered British 1st Division.

Kesselring and Mackensen discussed the possible approaches to eliminating the beachhead. An attack along the coast in the northern sector was judged to be impractical due to the immediate presence of Allied naval gunfire, nor was the approach along the coast on the southern flank much better. Instead, they concluded that an attack down the Via Anziate held most promise, with an aim towards splitting the

BATTLE FOR THE THUMB 3–11 FEBRUARY 1944

Between 3 February and 10 February, Allied units suffer heavy attacks, withdrawing from 'The Thumb' and losing control of both Aprilia, 'The Factory', and Carroceto station.

Note: Gridlines are shown at intervals of 1 Kilometer

PENNEY

OSTERIACCIA

CAMPOLEONE STATION

TUFELLO

ALLIED DEFENSE LINE 3 FEBURARY

DISUSED RAILWAY

ALLIED DEFENSE LINE FEBURARY

MOLETTA RIVER

ALLIED DEFENSE LINE 11 FEBURARY

▼ EVENTS

1. 2300 HOURS, 3 FEBRUARY, **Gruppe West** begins to infiltrate to the rear of the 3 Infantry Brigade positions near Campoleone Station while Gruppe Ost begins similar efforts on the eastern side of 'The Thumb'.

2. 0600, 4 FEBRUARY, German troops have broken through in small groups as far as the Via Anziate and begin heavy attacks against the 24 Guards Brigade units

3. 1600 HOURS, 4 FEBRUARY, German attacks nearly isolate the 3 Infantry Brigade from the 24 Guards Brigade, prompting Gen. Penney to stage a counterattack by the 168 Brigade using the 1 London Scottish, supported by two squadrons of 46 RTR tanks. By 1700, the gap is closed.

4. 1800 HOURS, 4 FEBRUARY. The vulnerability of the 3 Infantry Brigade prompts Penney to order a withdrawal back from 'The Thumb' after dark. The 1 Division loses about 1,400 troops in the day's fighting, mainly in the 24 Guards Brigade.

5. 1800 HOURS, 4 FEBRUARY, **3/504th** Parachute Infantry are brought up behind Carroceto Station to serve as a reserve.

6. 2100 HOURS, 7 FEBRUARY, German attacks resume with heavy artillery preparation against the flanks of the 1 Division. German troops begin to infiltrate 24 Guard Brigade positions along Buonriposa ridge.

7. 2400 HOURS, 7 FEBRUARY, general German attack begins and German 71st Infantry Division conducts limited attacks against right flank of 1 Division to tie down the 2 Infantry Brigade.

PFEIFFER

8. 0030 HOURS, 8 FEBRUARY, **the GR 145** attacks between 5 Grenadier and 2 N. Staffs defense line and by dawn both battalions have been pushed off the ridge after suffering heavy losses.

9. 0600 HOURS, 8 FEBRUARY, **limited attacks** by KG Gräser continue towards The Factory after earlier infiltration attempts. But tough defense by the 10 Berkshire and effective artillery support force a postponement of the main attack by a day.

10. 1330 HOURS, 8 FEBRUARY, **Penney** decides to counter-attack penetration by GR 145 on Buonriposa ridge by KSLI and Sherwood Foresters supported by a tank squadron from the 46 RTR. Small gains are made for stiff losses and counter-attack is halted after heavy rain complicates attack.

11. 0030 HOURS, 9 FEBRUARY, **after** reorganizing and reinforcing its attack force into two battle-groups, 3rd Panzer Grenadier Division renews the attacks for the Factory with KG Gräser to the east and KG Schönfeld to the west pushing directly for the factory.

12. 0030 HOURS, 9 FEBRUARY, **KG Pleiffer** continues its attacks from the Buonriposa ridge against 24 Guards Brigade positions. The US 1/1st Armored Regiment counter-attacks with two light tank companies in mid-morning but attack falters in the mud. At noon, the 3/1st Armored attacks with a company of medium tanks.

EAGLES

13. 1300 HOURS, 9 FEBRUARY, **KG Schönfeld** has seized the Factory and in conjunction with KG Gräser has also pushed as far as the lateral road. Both sides rest and reorganize due to the heavy losses of the day's fighting.

14. 2400 HOURS, 9 FEBRUARY, **KG Pleiffer** and KG Gräser launch a concerted attack against the Scots Guards holding the Carroceto railroad station. First attack is beaten off with support from M10 tank destroyers of Co. B, 894th Tank Destroyer Battalion but attacks are repeated through the early morning hours of 10 February, gradually decimating the isolated battalion.

15. 1000 HOURS, 10 FEBRUARY, **Allied air** attacks postpone German capture of Carroceto station, but when a heavy overcast develops around 0945 hours, KG Pleiffer finally secures the station. The station is recaptured later in the day, but in the evening, it falls back into German hands after another attack from the east by KG Gräser.

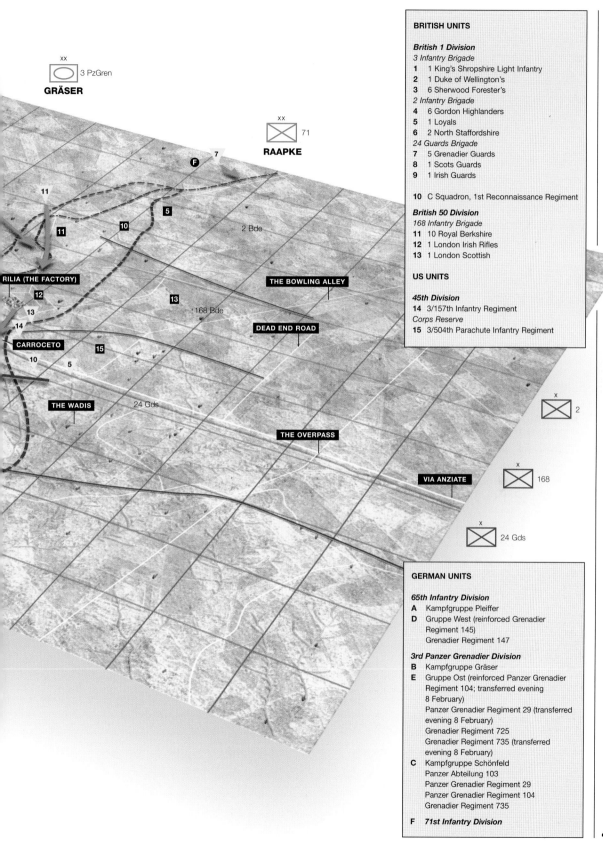

XX
3 PzGren
GRÄSER

XX
71
RAAPKE

7
F

11

5

10

11

10

2 Bde

RILIA (THE FACTORY)

12

13

THE BOWLING ALLEY

168 Bde

13

DEAD END ROAD

14

CARROCETO

15

10

5

THE WADIS

24 Gds

THE OVERPASS

x
2

VIA ANZIATE

x
168

x
24 Gds

BRITISH UNITS

British 1 Division
3 Infantry Brigade
1   1 King's Shropshire Light Infantry
2   1 Duke of Wellington's
3   6 Sherwood Forester's
2 Infantry Brigade
4   6 Gordon Highlanders
5   1 Loyals
6   2 North Staffordshire
24 Guards Brigade
7   5 Grenadier Guards
8   1 Scots Guards
9   1 Irish Guards

10 C Squadron, 1st Reconnaissance Regiment

British 50 Division
168 Infantry Brigade
11 10 Royal Berkshire
12 1 London Irish Rifles
13 1 London Scottish

US UNITS

45th Division
14 3/157th Infantry Regiment
Corps Reserve
15 3/504th Parachute Infantry Regiment

GERMAN UNITS

65th Infantry Division
A   Kampfgruppe Pleiffer
D   Gruppe West (reinforced Grenadier
        Regiment 145)
        Grenadier Regiment 147

3rd Panzer Grenadier Division
B   Kampfgruppe Gräser
E   Gruppe Ost (reinforced Panzer Grenadier
        Regiment 104; transferred evening
        8 February)
        Panzer Grenadier Regiment 29 (transferred
        evening 8 February)
        Grenadier Regiment 725
        Grenadier Regiment 735 (transferred
        evening 8 February)
C   Kampfgruppe Schönfeld
        Panzer Abteilung 103
        Panzer Grenadier Regiment 29
        Panzer Grenadier Regiment 104
        Grenadier Regiment 735

F   *71st Infantry Division*

47

Allied beachhead in two by a drive to the sea, followed by an elimination of the two halves. The delayed counter attack was rescheduled for 4 February once the fighting from the Allied offensive had petered out. Mackensen felt that Kesselring underestimated the problems faced by the 14th Army in eliminating the beachhead, particularly the mediocre quality of its inexperienced troops compared to the veteran units of the 10th Army on the Gustav line.

THE BATTLE OF THE THUMB

Mackensen's initial offensive was aimed at eliminating the salient created by the British 1st Division along the Via Anziate, nicknamed "the Thumb." The first attack was intended to reach limited objectives and to exploit Allied losses suffered in their offensive. Gruppe West consisted of the reinforced GR 145 from the 65th Division with the support of ten Hornisse self-propelled 88mm tank destroyers. Gruppe Ost consisted of PzGr Regt 104 with eight Hornisse. The attack began at 2300 hours on 3 February under heavy rain. The attack was intended to cut off the 3rd Infantry Brigade which was in the most exposed positions near Campoleone station. By dawn, the German attack had penetrated through the 24th Guards Brigade positions and reached the Via Anziate. Bitter fighting continued through most of the day as the Germans tried to secure their breakthrough while at the same time, the British infantry attempted to relieve the 3rd Brigade. Finally in the afternoon, Gen Penney ordered a counter attack by the 1st London Scottish from 168th Brigade, supported by Sherman tanks of the 46th RTR. Although the attack managed to close the gap, Penney realized that the 3rd Brigade positions were untenable and at 1800 hours, he ordered a general withdrawal of both the 3rd Brigade and 24th Guards Brigade out of "the Thumb" and back 4km to a more defensible line centered around "The Factory". By the end of the day, the 1st Division had suffered 1,400

A column from the British 1st Division move along the Via Anziate from Peter Beach on 22 January 1944. (NARA)

48

Paratroopers of the 504th Parachute Infantry Regiment with their distinctive baggy trousers carry a sniper casualty to a waiting ambulance on 24 January 1944. (NARA)

casualties, including the 920 captured in the fighting, mainly from the 3rd Brigade. German casualties were about 730 of whom about 300 had been captured. The newly arrived 168th Brigade from the 56th Division replaced the decimated 3rd Infantry Brigade. As a result, the reorganized defenses in this sector included three infantry brigades: the 24th Guards Brigade west of the Carroceto station, the 168th Infantry Brigade in the center and the 2nd Brigade to the east with the 3rd Brigade in reserve. The US 504th Parachute Infantry Regiment was shifted into this sector to serve as a reserve, stationed on the Via Anziate.

Mackensen renewed the attack on the night of 7–8 February with an aim to capture Carroceto and "The Factory." After feints in several sectors, KG Pleiffer (GR 145, 65th Infantry Division) staged a preliminary assault from the eastern side and KG Gräser (PzGren. Regt 29) on the western side. The German tactics were to infiltrate detachments through the British defenses under the cover of fog and darkness and set up resistance pockets in the rear, enabling them to bring the defenses under fire from all directions once the main attack began. The GR 145 successfully employed these tactics in the fighting with 24th Guards Brigade but the confused night battle ended in bitter hand-to-hand fighting with only modest gains for the attackers. KG Gräser was less successful and German losses had been so heavy in the night fighting that the main attack scheduled for dawn of 8 February had to be postponed until the night of 8–9 February. Intense fighting continued around "The Factory" during the day and Gen Penney was obliged to commit his reserve, the 3rd Brigade in the afternoon, mainly to reinforce the badly exposed 2nd North Staffords along the Buonriposo ridge

An M7 105mm howitzer motor carriage named *Anna* of Battery A, 69th Armored Field Artillery Battalion, 1st Armored Division in firing position near Nettuno on 2 February 1944. There are numerous empty ammunition packing tubes near the howitzer from heavy firing. (NARA)

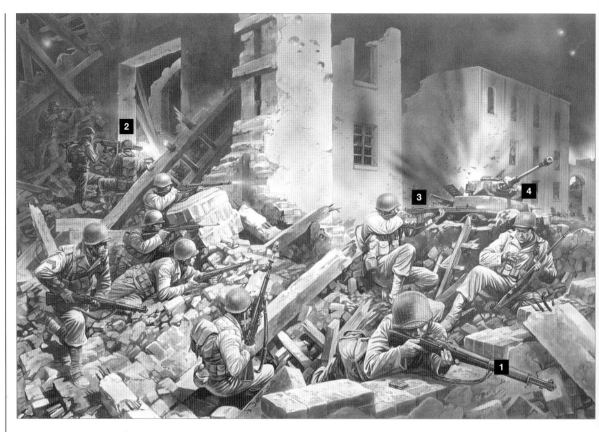

FIGHTING FOR 'THE FACTORY', 11 FEBRUARY 1944
(pages 50–51)

In the morning of 11 February, the 1st Battalion, 179th Infantry Regiment of the US 45th Division fought its way into the village of Aprilia, better known to the Allies as 'The Factory'. Kampfgruppe Gräser had wrested control of the Factory from the British 1 Division, and the 11 February attack was a last-gasp effort by Lucas to retain control over this critical road junction. The 1 Division had been so badly decimated in the previous fighting that Lucas was obliged to commit his reserve, the 45th Division, in the hopes of the holding the defensive line along Via Anziate. The German defenders, mainly from Grenadier Regiment 725, expected the Allies to try to retake the village. Company B, 1st Battalion, managed to fight its way into the south-eastern corner of the Factory by mid-day. But Aprilia was equally vital to Mackensen's plans for future attacks, and Kampfgruppe Gräser launched repeated attacks against the embattled US infantry through the night, culminating in an early morning panzer attack that flattened the buildings being used by the US troops for defense. The 1st Battalion was forced to withdraw after having lost about two thirds its troops. This scene depicts fighting within 'The Factory' by the 1/179th Infantry. The squad seen here is armed with

the typical assortment of US infantry weapons of the period. The basic weapon was the M1 Garand .30 caliber rifle, (1) one of the best weapons of its day. Unlike the bolt-action Kar. 98 used by the German infantry, the Garand was semi-automatic, providing a faster rate of fire. This was not a decisive advantage, though, as the Germans used different infantry tactics. The German infantry based its tactics around its automatic weapons, principally the MG-34 or MG-42 light machine gun. The light machine gun, (2) with a very high rate of fire, provided the base of fire for the squad, and the riflemen supported the machine gun team. The US squad had its own automatic weapon, the BAR Browning Automatic Rifle (3). But it was magazine fed rather than belt-fed, giving it a slower rate of fire. US infantry tactics placed greater emphasis on aimed fire from the individual rifleman, rather than concentrating on their automatic weapons. The knocked out tank in the background is a PzKpfw IV (4), the workhorse of the Wehrmacht panzer force in 1943-44. Even if the terrain was far from ideal for tank operations, both sides made frequent use of tanks at Anzio, principally in the infantry support role. During the fighting for the Factory on 11–12 April, the 179th Infantry was supported by M4 medium tanks of the 191st Tank Battalion.
(Peter Dennis)

The 1st and 3rd Ranger Battalions were wiped out during their attempt to infiltrate into Cisterna, seen in the far upper right of this photo. They advanced along the Pantano ditch, part of which is visible to the upper right where it intersects Highway 7. The ruins of Isola Bella are evident in the foreground, and the Alban hills in the background. (MHI)

A pair of Sherman III tanks of the 46th RTR supporting the British 1st Division along the Anzio beachhead in early February 1944. (NARA)

who by this stage of the fighting had suffered 50 percent casualties. The Germans captured 791 British prisoners, mainly from the 5th Grenadier Guards, 2nd North Staffords and the 1st Irish Guards, and the fighting quietened down in the afternoon as both sides attempted to reorganize.

Another major attack was launched at midnight, taking advantage of the gains made during the previous day's fighting, and committing about six infantry regiments to the struggle. The strongest assault was conducted by KG Gräser against the 168th Brigade. Tank companies from the US 1st Armored Regiment were sent in piecemeal to reinforce the British positions during the morning, but the area was so muddy after the incessant winter rain that the tanks quickly became bogged down once they moved off the roads. The repeated German attacks gradually pushed the British infantry out of "The Factory." By the afternoon, both sides were exhausted and the British 1st Division was barely holding after it had been reduced by constant fighting to half strength. The Fifth Army G-3 operations officer recommended committing the only infantry reserve, the 45th Division, to hold the line. After continued night fighting Gen Penney reported at dawn that the 1st Division would be unable to hold the line without a counter attack by fresh troops. Two further German infantry assaults against the Carroceto railroad station were broken up by a concentrated artillery barrage, and Allied tactical air support intervened for a few hours in the morning before overcast rolled in after 0945 hours preventing further air sorties. An Allied counterattack managed to recapture

OPERATION FISCHFANG, 16–20 FEBRUARY 1944

Initial Axis attacks fail to make much headway and a series of attacks and counter-attacks finally ends in stalemate, largely due to the effectiveness of Allied artillery.

Note: Gridlines are shown at intervals of 1 Kilometer

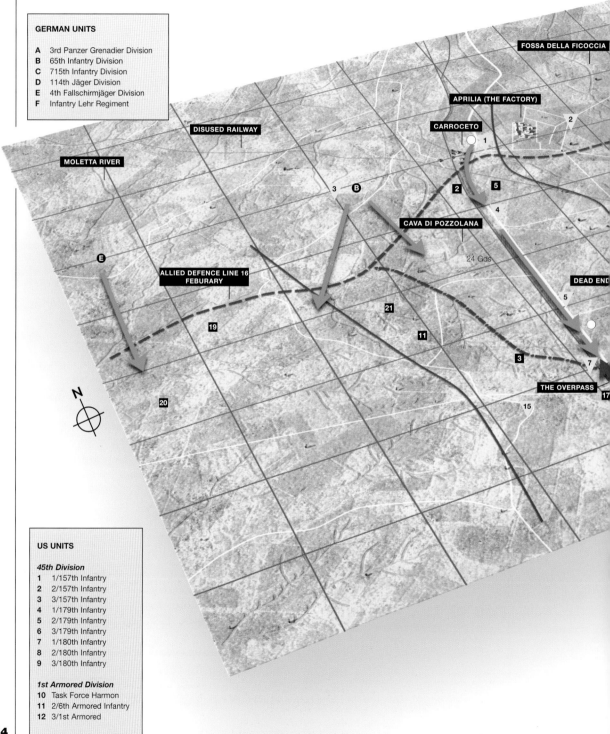

GERMAN UNITS

A 3rd Panzer Grenadier Division
B 65th Infantry Division
C 715th Infantry Division
D 114th Jäger Division
E 4th Fallschirmjäger Division
F Infantry Lehr Regiment

FOSSA DELLA FICOCCIA

APRILIA (THE FACTORY)

DISUSED RAILWAY

CARROCETO

MOLETTA RIVER

CAVA DI POZZOLANA

24 Gds

ALLIED DEFENCE LINE 16 FEBURARY

DEAD END

THE OVERPASS

US UNITS

45th Division
1 1/157th Infantry
2 2/157th Infantry
3 3/157th Infantry
4 1/179th Infantry
5 2/179th Infantry
6 3/179th Infantry
7 1/180th Infantry
8 2/180th Infantry
9 3/180th Infantry

1st Armored Division
10 Task Force Harmon
11 2/6th Armored Infantry
12 3/1st Armored

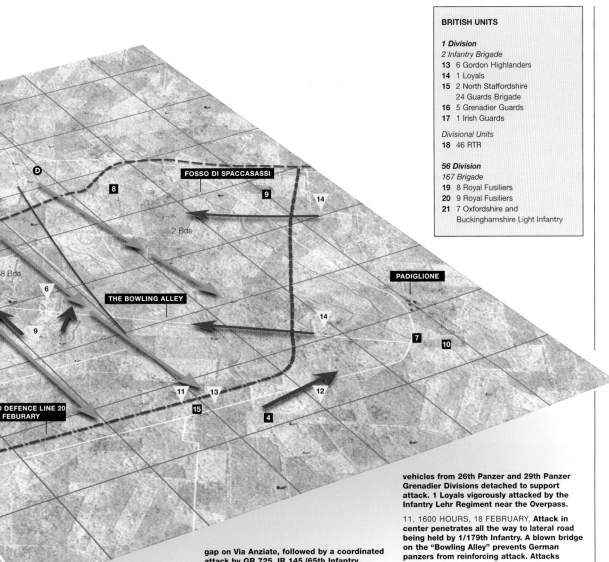

FOSSO DI SPACCASASSI

2 Bde

8 Bde

THE BOWLING ALLEY

PADIGLIONE

DEFENCE LINE 20
FEBURARY

EVENTS

1. 0600 HOURS 16 FEBRUARY, **Operation Fischfang begins with preliminary artillery bombardment.**

2. 0730 HOURS, 16 FEBRUARY, **3rd Panzer Grenadier Division advances on the west of the attack axis, 715th Infantry Division on the right, but initial attacks fail to make much headway into American defenses**

3. 0730 HOURS, 16 FEBRUARY, diversionary attacks are launched along the whole front, including attacks by the 65th Infantry Division over the Buonriposa ridge.

4. 2300 HOURS, 16 FEBRUARY, **GR 725 of the 715th Infantry Division infiltrates positions of the 2/157th Infantry on Via Anziate, creating a gap with neighboring 2/179th Infantry by dawn.**

5. 0740 HOURS, 17 FEBRUARY, **the Luftwaffe stages an air attack by 35 fighters along the**

gap on Via Anziate, followed by a coordinated attack by GR 725, IR 145 (65th Infantry Division) and elements of IR 741 (114th Jäger Division). By mid-morning, a deep salient is created down the Via Anziate.

6. 1200 HOURS, 17 FEBRUARY, **3rd Panzer Grenadier Division pushes along perimeter held by the 2nd and 3rd Battalions, 179th Infantry, opening up a salient down towards the lateral road and disused railway bed nicknamed "The Bowling Alley"**

7. 1200 HOURS, 17 FEBRUARY, **Co. H, 1st Armored Regiment dispatched to Overpass to help stop German advance, reaches the overpass around 1410 hours and pushes up Via Anziate. Co. I pushes up the Bowling Alley.**

8. 1500 HOURS, 17 FEBRUARY. **With German tanks penetrating near the Overpass, Lucas directs British 1 Division, the Corps reserve, to begin deploying its units south of the Overpass to block any German approach to the beach.**

9. 2300 HOURS, 17 FEBRUARY, **The 179th Infantry is ordered to counter-attack to restore lost ground but is mauled in the process worsening its position.**

10. 0630 HOURS, 18 FEBRUARY. **German attack resumed along whole front. Armored**

vehicles from 26th Panzer and 29th Panzer Grenadier Divisions detached to support attack. 1 Loyals vigorously attacked by the Infantry Lehr Regiment near the Overpass.

11. 1600 HOURS, 18 FEBRUARY, **Attack in center penetrates all the way to lateral road being held by 1/179th Infantry. A blown bridge on the "Bowling Alley" prevents German panzers from reinforcing attack. Attacks continue all through the salient until 2130 hours when Germans break off the fighting to reorganize.**

12. 2400 HOURS, 18 FEBRUARY. **The US 45th Division uses the lull to readjust its lines and reinforce forward units.**

13. 0400 HOURS, 19 FEBRUARY. **German artillery begins a preparatory bombardment followed by infantry attacks all along the perimeter of the salient at 0410. This attack is met by a prepared Allied artillery strike. The attacks continue all day, but fail to make any appreciable gains.**

14. 0630 HOURS, 19 FEBRUARY. **Task Force H with a battalion of M4 tanks and the 30th Infantry stages a counter-attack up the Bowling Alley and a parallel track to the northeast. Attack blunts German effort in the eastern sector, and halts at 1620.**

15. 0430 HOURS, 20 FEBRUARY. **Panzer Grenadier Regiment 67 of the 26th Panzer Division launches an attack against 1 Loyals but is badly beaten up by artillery before reaching Allied lines. Other attacks fail due to Allied artillery, or other problems. 14th Army has suffered to many casualties to continue attack with any vigor.**

Artillery was a key ingredient in all the fighting along the beachhead. This is a US 155mm gun in action near Nettuno on 13 February 1944. (NARA)

the Carroceto station, only to be forced out in the evening by KG Gräser. By the end of 10 February, the German offensive petered out, "the Thumb" had been eliminated, with both Buonriposo ridge and "The Factory" in German hands. Losses on both sides had been heavy, the worst hit being the British 168th Brigade which was barely at one-third strength. In the three days of fighting, the Germans captured 2,563 troops, nearly all from the 1st Division, which was at less than half strength: staggering losses for so short a period of time.

The 1st Division commander, Gen Penney, was indignant over Lucas' failure to grasp how precarious the situation around Carroceto had become. Lucas visited the front on the afternoon of 10 February and Penney convinced him of the need to shift fresh troops into the area and stage an immediate counter attack. Lucas ordered the US 45th Division to deploy two of its infantry regiments to retake "The Factory" and reinforce the decimated 1st Division. With the support of the 191st Tank Battalion, 1/179th Infantry from the 45th Division staged a counter attack against "The Factory" at dawn on 11 February, which was held by KG Gräser. The lead tanks managed to smash up the German defenses in the surviving buildings, but were forced to withdraw when they ran out of ammunition. The attack resumed in the early afternoon and the 1/179th Infantry fought its way into the southeast corner of "The Factory." They were forced out, and although a renewed attack in the late afternoon gained a foothold in the ruins, a German counterattack restored the defenses. The seesaw battle continued after dark with two companies from 1/179th Infantry fighting their way into "The Factory", only to

A 40mm Bofors anti-aircraft gun is deployed along the Anzio beach to defend against the frequent Luftwaffe air raids. (NARA)

Immediate fighter support for the beachhead was provided by the US 307th Fighter Squadron, based near Nettuno starting on 1 February. The squadron was equipped with Spitfire Mk IX, but was forced to abandon the base at Nettuno on 16 February due to frequent German artillery fire. (MHI)

be pushed out again around dawn by a German counter attack. By this stage, it had become evident that it would take a major effort to pry the German infantry out of "The Factory" and so the attacks were suspended. Instead, US heavy bombers dropped 145 tons of bombs on German reserves near Campoleone station and Cecchina. A temporary lull ensued over the next few days as both sides tried to recuperate from their heavy losses.

OPERATION *FISCHFANG*

Kesselring and Mackensen had expected to stage a broad offensive against the Anzio beachhead as soon as forces were sufficient, and Operation *Fischfang* (Fishing) was scheduled for 16 February. Hitler approved the plan on 11 February, believing that a decisive defeat of a major Allied amphibious landing would delay any Allied landing in France. Kesselring wanted two more divisions for the attack, which Hitler refused. Instead, he offered some new secret weapons as well as the Berlin–Spandau Infantry Lehr (Training) Regiment which he instructed be given a central assignment in the attack. The secret weapons included new remote control demolition vehicles, a company of the heavy 88mm Ferdinand tank destroyer, and a battalion with the new Panther tanks. Hitler also insisted on a World War I style creeping barrage, an order that was largely ignored as there was insufficient ammunition to carry it out. While the size of the opposing artillery forces was similar, 432 Allied guns versus 452 German guns, the available ammunition supply markedly favored the Allies. The main attack down Via Anziate would be conducted by the 1st Fallschirmjäger Corps, while the 76th Panzer Corps staged diversionary attacks against the US 3rd Division near Cisterna.

A German paratrooper squad takes a break in the shelter of a farm building during the fighting for the Anzio beachhead. (MHI)

57

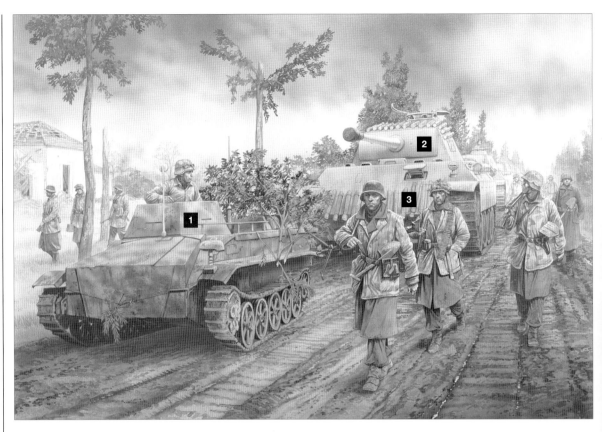

OPERATION FISCHFANG, 16 FEBRUARY 1944 (pages 58–59)

When Mackensen asked Hitler for another two divisions to attack the Anzio beach-head, he was instead promised several new secret weapons including remote control demolition vehicles and a battalion of the new Panther tank, both seeing their combat debut in the western theater at Anzio. The substitution of new wonder weapons for combat-experienced troops was symptomatic of the problems facing the Wehrmacht in 1944 and a foretaste of the continued decline in the Wehrmacht order of battle through 1944. The scene here depicts a column of infantry marching past an armored column to the rear of the battle-line during Operation Fischfang. The armored column is headed by one of the Borgward B-IV remote control demolition vehicles (1) of 3./s.Panzer Abteilung 504, followed by a column of Panther Ausf. A tanks (2) of Panzer Regiment 4. The B-IV demolition vehicle was a small, tank-like vehicle that had a small compartment for the operator in the front. Generally, the B-IV was driven close to the target area by the driver, but once within enemy small-arms range the driver would exit the vehicle and switch it to radio control. The B-IV was remotely controlled from a tank or armored vehicle, in this case by a specially equipped Tiger I tank of the third company of s.Pz.Abt. 504. The B-IV would be driven towards a vital target by remote control, and on reaching its destination, a wedged-shaped high-explosive container with 450 kg of high explosives on the nose of the vehicle would be jettisoned against the target. Once the B-IV had been withdrawn to a safe-distance, the charge was remotely detonated. While a good idea on paper, the B-IV proved awkward to use in combat conditions, particularly during Operation Fischfang due to the muddy conditions, which led to the vehicle becoming easily bogged down. In addition, there were few high-value targets when facing infantry in simple trenches. The Panther tank was also a disappointment at Anzio. The early production run had mechanical reliability problems which were compounded by the muddy conditions in February 1944 which kept the panzers road-bound. As a result, the new Panther battalion deployed at Anzio was restricted by the corps commander in the conduct of its operations. The high command did not wish to lose one of the new tanks to the Allies, so the battalion commander was instructed to keep his tanks back from the forward edge of battle and engage in long range fire only. These Panther tanks display a local innovation at Anzio, a type of simple anti-mud device consisting of small tree branches lashed together with wire or rope to create a length of matting.(3) If the tank became bogged down in the mud, the matting could be placed under one or both tracks to provide additional traction. The limitations of the new weapons at Anzio meant that the 'landsers' the common German infantrymen, bore the brunt of the fighting. Given the Allied superiority in artillery, the muddy fields, and the Allied trench-lines, it was a grim and costly business, with a high butcher's bill by the end of each of the German attacks.
(Peter Dennis)

German Forces, Operation *Fischfang*, 16 February 1944

14th Army — **Generaloberst Eberhard von Mackensen**
Panzer Division Hermann Göring — Generalleutnant Paul Conrath
26th Panzer Division — Generalmajor Hans Hecker
29th Panzergrenadier Division — General der Panzertruppen Walter Fries
1/Panzer Regiment 4 (Panther)
    s.Pz.Abt. 508 (Tiger)

1st Fallschirmjäger Corps
4th Fallschirmjäger Division — Generalmajor Heinrich Trettner
65th Infantry Division — Generalleutnant Hellmut Pfeiffer
Rome Kommendatura (Military police battalions)
Corps Units
    Pz.Gr.Regt. 1027
    s.PzJäger Abt. 590
    s.Pz.Jäger Abt. 525 (88mm Hornisse)
    StuG Abt., 11th Luftwaffe Corps
    Luftwaffe Engineer Battalion 22

76th Panzer Corps — **General der Infanterie Dietrich von Choltitz**
3rd Panzergrenadier Division — General der Panzertruppen Fritz-Hubert Gräser
114th Jäger Division — Generalleutnant Alexander Bourquin
715th Mot. Infantry Division — Generalleutnant Hans-Georg Hildebrandt
Corps Units
Infantry Lehr Regiment
Panzergrenadier Regiment 1028
    3/Fallschirmjäger Regt. 1
    Fallschirmjäger Lehr Battalion
    7th Luftwaffe Field Battalion
    2/SS Grenadier Regt. 35
    2/SS Grenadier Regt. 36
    Fusilier Battalion 362
    Sturmpanzer Abt. 216 (Brummbär)
    Funklenk Panzer Battalion 301
    Engineer Battalion 60
    Panzer Engineer Battalion 811
    Panzer Engineer Battalion 813

Infantry of the Irish Guards advance behind a Sherman III tank of the 46th RTR on the Via Anziate. (NARA)

German Artillery Strength for Operation *Fischfang*, 16 February 1944

105mm howitzer	114
150mm howitzer	46
100mm gun	39
170mm gun	6
210mm howitzer	3
210mm railway gun	2
240mm railway gun	2
150mm multiple rocket launcher	54
210mm multiple rocket launcher	14
88mm anti-aircraft gun	172
Total	**452**

Operation *Fischfang* began on 16 February 1944 under clear skies, but with the fields a morass of mud after days of relentless winter rain. A 30-minute counter-battery artillery preparation started before dawn at 0600 hours. The main attack was concentrated along Via Anziate, coinciding closely with the six-mile sector held by the US 45th Division. The spearheads of the attack were the 3rd Panzergrenadier Division and 715th Infantry Division attacking the positions of the 157th and 179th Infantry, roughly a three-to-one force ratio in the attack sector. In spite of their numerical superiority, the German infantry faced heavy US artillery fire, and in particular the 179th Infantry had an artillery forward observer in a farmhouse opposite "The Factory" who was able to call in particularly accurate fire. Some technical novelties were brought forward for the attack, including two Panzer battalions equipped with remote control demolition vehicles. These small tracked vehicles were filled with high explosive, and were remotely controlled towards high value targets and then remotely detonated. In the event, they proved almost totally ineffective as they often got bogged down in the muddy ground.

The German infantry assaults were supported by Panzers that would sally out of "The Factory," pummel US trenches with gunfire, and then return to "The Factory" to replenish their ammunition. Casualties on both sides in the morning fighting were very heavy, and the inexperienced Infantry Lehr Regiment, attached to the 3rd Panzergrenadier Division for the attack, fled in disorder in the early afternoon after losing most of their

A pair of Grille 150mm self-propelled howitzers and a SdKfz 251 Ausf C halftrack from the 3rd Panzergrenadier Division use the demolished buildings of Carroceto for cover. The knocked-out British Sherman III tank, probably from the 46th RTR, rests near the San Antonio chapel and in the background can be seen "The Factory." (MHI)

One of the innovations deployed against the Anzio bridgehead were the Borgward B.IV remote control demolition vehicles serving with Panzer Abt. (FkI) 301. These carried a large high explosive charge that was dropped off against the target, and then the vehicle was remotely controlled back to safety before the charge detonated. These vehicles did not prove very effective at Anzio and this example is being examined by British officers on 20 April 1944. (NARA)

officers and NCOs. By noon, the 179th Infantry was being supported by 144 guns around the Anzio perimeter, as well as direct fire support from the 645th Tank Destroyer Battalion and a company from the 191st Tank Battalion. The 3rd Panzergrenadier Division had fought in the Stalingrad campaign, and prisoners taken from the division complained that the fighting at Anzio, particularly the artillery onslaught, was worse than anything they had ever seen in Russia.

German artillery support against the 157th Infantry was more prolonged and intense than in other sectors, so the infantry assault did not begin until 0730 hours. Once again, the infantry attacks were closely supported by Panzers, but the German armor suffered significant losses from attached tank destroyers. The muddy terrain limited the effectiveness of the Panzers, which became trapped as soon as they ventured off the road.

While the main attack was being conducted against the 45th Division, diversionary attacks were launched against the US 3rd Division and the British 56th Division. These attacks were smaller in size, ranging from platoons to a few companies and widely scattered along the whole perimeter. The most intense attack was conducted by the Fallschirmjäger Lehr Battalion supported by nine PzKpfw IV tanks of the Panzer Division Hermann Göring against the US 3rd Division. Two companies of the paratroopers were virtually wiped out by artillery fire. The British 56th Division was hit by the 3/Sturm Regt. 12, and there were some penetrations of the infantry defenses that were mopped up by the supporting Sherman tanks of the 46th RTR. By the evening of the first day, Operation *Fischfang* had failed to make any significant penetrations in the defenses. German casualties totaled 324 killed, 1,207 wounded and 146 missing, the heaviest German casualties yet of the Anzio campaign.

The German attacks resumed around midnight, with KG Gräser trying to infiltrate the 157th Infantry positions on the Via Anziate. These tactics were successful and before dawn, a gap was opening between the 157th and 179th infantry. The US 45th Division was struck by a particularly heavy air attack after dawn, followed by an assault by three German regiments, GR 725, GR 145 and GR 741, supported by about sixty tanks. The intense German attack pushed the 45th Division back along a front two miles wide and a mile deep. The VI Corps responded by concentrating its artillery on the German positions, supported by naval gun fire, 90mm anti-aircraft guns and three companies of tanks from the 1st Armored Division. The XII Air Support Command flew 198 fighter-bomber, 69 light-bomber, 176 medium-bomber and 288 heavy-bomber missions in support of the corps that day.

The appalling casualties suffered by the German assault troops forced Mackensen to rotate units through the front. In the afternoon, it was the turn of the 3rd Panzergrenadier Division to try to broaden the penetration with renewed attacks. Many German infantry battalions had

A US mortar team block their ears to protect against the sharp report of their 60mm mortar during fighting along the Anzio perimeter. (NARA)

Much of the fighting in the center of the bridgehead was fought around the village of Aprilia, better known to the Allied troops as "The Factory": a complex of substantial buildings created in the interwar years as a model Fascist farming community. The Via Anziate can be seen snaking to the left and the Albano hills are evident in the background. (MHI)

been reduced to 125–150 men, about a quarter of their strength, due to a ferocious pummeling by Allied artillery. The German commanders had expected to be able to reinforce their attack with their considerable Panzer reserves, but the ground was so wet and soggy that the Panzers were limited to the roads. The German penetration became so serious that Lucas ordered the battered British 1st Division, in reserve after its heavy losses earlier in the month, to deploy along a prepared defense line behind the 45th Division. During the deployment, the 1st Division commander, Gen Penney, was wounded by an artillery fragment.

After nightfall, Gen Eagles of the 45th Division ordered a counter-attack by the 2nd and 3rd Battalions, 157th Infantry and the 3/179th Infantry. These battalions had been badly worn down by the fighting, with under 300 men each out of an original strength of about 870 men. These attacks did not have enough strength to succeed and only managed to further weaken the 179th Infantry defenses. The counter attack did not prevent the Germans from infiltrating assault detachments through US lines. The renewed German attacks on the morning of 18 February included elements of five infantry regiments. Mackensen had hoped to reserve his two best division , the 26th Panzer Division and 29th Panzergrenadier Divisions for a final lunge for the sea, but instead he was forced to commit them to the breakthrough operation due to the heavy casualties in the initial attack force. The 179th Infantry, depleted by the night attack, was particularly hard hit. The morning attack pushed deeper into the American defenses, but the shoulders continued to hold in spite of the losses, with the 2/157th Infantry holed up in caves to the west of Via Anziate. One of the few British 1st Division battalions to have avoided the carnage of the Battle for the Thumb, the 1st Loyals, was positioned on Via Anziate at a railroad overpass, variously called the "First Overpass" or "Flyover" by the Allied troops. The battalion was hit full force by the Lehr Regiment, hoping to redeem its reputation after its disgraceful performance the first day of the offensive. At the center of the Allied positions, the 1st Loyals continued to resist repeated onslaughts until the Germans finally gave up in the afternoon and redirected the focus of their attack on the 180th Infantry. Allied artillery continued to have a devastating impact on the German infantry. Shortly before noon, a divisional spotter plane observed one of the German regiments moving forward with about 2,500 troops. Within 12 minutes, the Corps artillery was able to concentrate 224 British and US guns on the regiment and smashed it before it could begin its attack. Col. William Darby, commander of the decimated Ranger force, was sent to command the beleaguered 179th Infantry in the early afternoon.

In the late afternoon, the Germans renewed the attacks along the front, with Panzers supporting the attacks along the Via Anziate, and the "Bowling Alley" road. Although some advances were made, the attacks petered out after nightfall due to the exhaustion on both sides. The US 45th Division, which had taken the brunt of the assault, was reinforced with divisional reserves and by stripping personnel out of rear area units to replace the heavy casualties in the infantry companies. The German 715th Infantry Division had suffered such heavy losses in the attack that it was withdrawn. During the night of 18–19 February, Mackensen ordered divisions not heavily committed to the assault to give up individual infantry battalions which were transferred to the assault force for a renewed attack the following morning. The scale of German losses on 18 February were never accurately tallied as the three divisions that bore the brunt of the attack, the 114th Jäger, 29th Panzergrenadier and 715th Infantry, were in no position to report, but the butcher's bill was undoubtedly grim.

The fighting on 19 February started before dawn with an intense German barrage along the front with especially heavy infantry attacks against the 179th Infantry, and the 1st Loyals. Allied artillery played a significant role in breaking up the attacks, and, after the heavy casualties of the previous fighting, the German dawn attack by the 65th Infantry Division began to falter. Lucas had ordered the formation of a counter attack force to attempt to regain the area lost over the

A group of German prisoners from the 114th Jäger Division captured near Carroceto during the fighting on 19 February 1944.

A patrol brings back prisoners near Carroceto on 19 February. Of interest is the proximity of the GI trenches to the irrigation ditch. The low water table around the beachhead led to chronic problems of flooded foxholes and trenchfoot. (NARA)

A pair of A-20 bombers encounter flak over Cisterna during a mission there on 29 February 1944. (NARA)

previous day's fighting. Force T under Gen Templer was formed from the newly arrived British 169th Brigade while Force H under General Harmon of the 1st Armored Division was based around the 6th Armored Infantry (1st Armored Division), the 30th Infantry (3rd Division), and a battalion of medium tanks. Force T was unable to start the attack as planned due to equipment still tied up in the port. Force H began its attack at 0630 hours following a heavy artillery preparation. The attack penetrated more than a mile into German lines and by the middle of the afternoon had succeeded in disrupting any further attacks by the 114th Jäger Division on the eastern side of the salient.

By the end of 19 February, Lucas realized that the Germans were a spent force. The prisoners being taken came from a bewildering number of different units, cobbled together as a desperate final attempt to break through the Allied lines. The final attacks, launched the next morning, were a pale shadow of the earlier assaults. A company strength attack against the 1st Loyals in the pre-dawn hours was quickly beaten back. The 29th Panzergrenadier Division, which had been assigned the main missions of the day, launched a confused attack before dawn but failed communications forced the attacking regiments to withdraw in disorder even before reaching Allied lines. This was the last major assault of Operation *Fischfang*.

German casualties during Operation *Fischfang* were at least 5,389 killed, wounded and missing of whom 609 were captured by the Allies. In reality, the total was significantly higher, but some German units were so badly decimated that many casualty reports were never compiled. On 19 February, the strength of the 65th Infantry Division was only 901 men, less than a tenth of its nominal strength. Mackensen attributed three-quarters of the German casualties to the Allied artillery. The main Allied advantage had been in ammunition supplies rather than in the number of guns, and Allied commanders estimated that at the peak of the fighting on 18–19 February, the Allied artillery was firing 15–20 rounds for every German artillery round, finally totaling some 158,000 rounds during 17–20 February. German infantry commanders were particularly bitter over the lack of Panzer support which was caused by the wet weather and soggy ground, and not the availability of tanks of which there had been an ample supply. The conditions were so bad that the new Panther battalion sent to Anzio was kept in reserve or used for long-range firing rather than risk untimely capture of one of these new tanks.

Allied casualties were at least 3,496 killed, wounded and missing of which 1,304 had been captured by the Germans, but records were so spotty that the actual totals were probably higher. The Allies also suffered 1,637 non-battle casualties, mainly due to trenchfoot in the water-logged foxholes.

Among the casualties of the offensive was Gen Lucas, who was relieved by Gen Alexander on 22 February and replaced by the 3rd Division commander, Lucian Truscott. Lucas was relieved "without prejudice" and Alexander made it clear that he felt that Lucas was simply too exhausted and demoralized to remain in command. In many respects, Lucas was a scapegoat for the failure of a confused and poorly conceived operation. Lucas had made clear his objections to the operation from the outset and if Alexander and Clark had actually expected bold action, their choice of Lucas was a poor one. Truscott was a younger and more dynamic commander than Lucas at a time when the troops needed a more visible and vigorous command presence. Relations between Lucas and the British commanders, especially Gen Penney were at a low ebb, and Truscott's efforts restored British confidence.

Although Operation *Shingle* had failed in its primary intent of breaking the stalemate in Italy, it contributed to the overall strategic goal of the Allied campaign in Italy of tying down German divisions. It lured Hitler into shifting more units into Italy than otherwise would have been the case, and weakened the forces of the 10th Army along the Gustav line

Two GIs of the 1st Special Service Force mark the grave of a German solider on 28 February 1944. (NARA)

at a time when further reinforcement was becoming more and more unlikely. Berlin assumed that the Allies would land in France within three months, and a major summer offensive by the Red Army was inevitable. Hitler could no longer afford to send major reinforcements to Italy when they were badly needed in more important theaters. Kesselring now had to defend a more extended main line of resistance with fewer and fewer troops of poorer and poorer quality. Anzio did not have the sudden and dramatic effect that was intended, but in the longer term, it placed a continuing strain on limited German resources, gradually corroding Kesselring's defenses.

OPERATION *SEITENSPRUNG*

Even though Operation *Fischfang* had failed, Kesselring was not willing to halt attempts to crush the Anzio beachhead. He realized that time was not in his favor, and unless Anzio was stamped out quickly, the Allies would continue to reinforce the beachhead. However, losses had been so high, and the process of reinforcement of the assault forces so improvised that it would take at least a week to straighten out the forward units of the 14th Army before renewing the attacks. In the interim, Mackensen was ordered to continue limited attacks until the main assault was ready. Fighting persisted along the western shoulder of the salient where surviving elements of the 2/157th Infantry were surrounded and trapped in caves. Force Templer reached the cut-off unit on the night of 21 February, but German resistance was still so determined that in the end the positions had to be abandoned. Other German units continued to attempt to nibble away at exposed Allied defenses, but the fighting was on a small scale compared to the previous week's combat.

Mackensen planned to renew the assault on 29 February, codenamed Operation *Seitensprung* (Escapade), primarily against the US 3rd Infantry Division along the eastern shoulder of the salient. The German

The Luftwaffe was very active over the Anzio beachhead, and a common weapon used against Allied troops was the AB500-1, a cluster bomb containing 37 SD-10 smaller submunitions. This is the empty case after the payload was dispensed. (NARA)

Anzio was subjected to long-range bombardment by the railroad guns of the Erhart railroad artillery battery, with the long range 280mm guns being dubbed "Anzio Annie" by US troops. One of these Krupp 280mm K5(E) guns named *Leopold* was captured in the rail-yard at Civitavecchia and subsequently shipped back to the US where it currently resides at the Ordnance Museum at Aberdeen Proving Ground. (NARA)

During the frequent artillery
duels around the beachhead,
both sides used anti-aircraft
artillery in a field artillery role.
This 90mm anti-aircraft gun of
Battery C, 68th Coast Artillery
(AAA) is seen in action
on 9 March 1944. (NARA)

14th Army had nine divisions facing the five divisions of the VI Corps, with five of these concentrated against the US 3rd Division. However, the divisional total obscures the fact that the German divisions were badly under-strength due to the February casualties, so that the actual combat strength of both sides was more nearly equal than the divisional total would suggest. The focus of the attack was from Carano towards Isola Bella, though a diversionary attack against the British 56th Division on the western shoulder was also planned.

On the afternoon of 28 February, the 14th Army began laying smoke along the front lines to mask final preparations for the attack. The VI Corps expected an attack, and reinforced the 3rd Division with two self-

The crew of a British 4.2in
mortar of the 2nd Infantry
Brigade Support Group prepare
their weapon during the fighting
on 15 March 1944. (MHI)

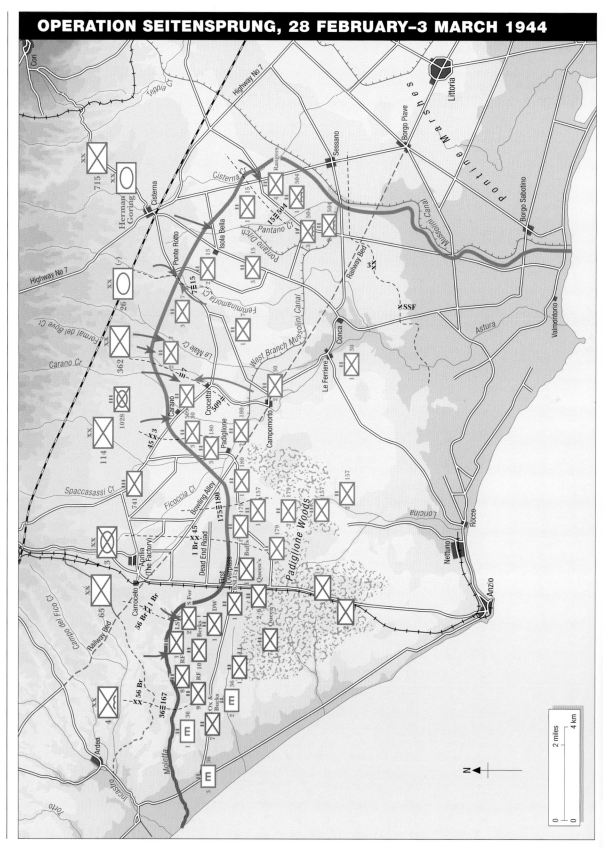

An M10 3-in GMC from a tank destroyer battalion supporting the US 3rd Division. The beachhead was so open that any cover available was used for concealment, in this case, a haystack. (NARA)

A couple of GIs service their .30cal light machine gun in a farm building while under the protection of an M4 medium tank.

propelled howitzer battalions. When the 14th Army began its preparatory bombardment on the morning of 29 February, the VI Corps answered in kind with its own barrage. Most of the German attacks were smashed by artillery and small arms fire. One of the few to make any significant penetration was the assault by Pz.Gren.Regt. 1028 and units of the 362nd Infantry Division which hit the 509th Parachute Battalion on the road towards Carano. The attack was reminiscent of World War I with German pioneers leading the attack with wire cutters and Bangalore torpedoes to breach the barbed wire, followed by shouting and singing infantry. The assault overwhelmed one paratrooper company and penetrated into the American defenses to the battalions' supporting mortar platoons. The mortar crews fought off the attack with rifles as well as mortar fire, and Company A established a new defense line. Although the assault had penetrated 800 meters into the American lines, it was stalled and the lead German units were under heavy fire. The supporting attack to the west by 2/Pz.Gren.Regt. 1028 was caught up in the barbed wire and both early morning attacks were halted after the lead officers were killed. The 362nd Infantry Division tried to widen the breach on the eastern side against the 2/7th Infantry, but was pummeled by artillery and mortar fire. By the afternoon, the German attacks had completely stalled and, after dark, the 2/30th Infantry counter-attacked to regain the small salient that had been taken. There were additional company and battalion-sized attacks, including several supported by Panzers during the course of the day, but they failed to make any significant penetrations of the Allied defenses. German casualties during the attack were over 900

killed, wounded and missing for practically no gains. The 14th Army estimated they had been hit by 66,000 rounds of artillery, about double the fire of Allied artillery during Operation *Fischfang*. The only solace was that the weather had been so miserable that it had prevented the intervention of Allied air power.

The German attacks were repeated on 1 March but on a reduced scale due to the previous day's losses. Fighting continued against the small salient around Carano, with the US 2/30th Infantry regaining the lost territory by 0830 hours. The most intense fighting of the day centered around some PzKpfw IV and Tiger tanks from the 26th Panzer Division which had captured a bridge southwest of Ponte Rotto the previous day in the 7th Infantry sector. During the pre-dawn hours, the 7th Infantry tried to illuminate the area with flares to make the Panzers visible to nearby tank destroyers, but the pouring rain squelched the flares. The Panzers

The Allied positions around Anzio were so exposed to German observation from the Alban hills that various methods of deception had to be used to mask troop deployments. This type of inflatable Sherman tank was deployed by British forces to deceive the Germans regarding actual force locations. (NARA)

Due to the flat terrain around most of the beachhead, a preferred German tactic was to infiltrate Allied lines under the cover of dark or early morning fog using the shallow irrigation ditches. This grim image records how costly this tactic could be if the infiltrating troops were discovered. (NARA)

Allied positions in the beachhead were exposed to the view of German artillery observers in the Alban hills, so the Allies frequently resorted to the use of smoke to cloak tactical movements prior to operations as seen here on 22 March 1944 with a generator of the 179th Chemical Smoke Battalion. (NARA)

The 34th Division arrived in the beachhead at the end of March and replaced the 3rd Division on the line. Here a newly arrived 34th Division platoon moves forward. (NARA)

responded by blasting one platoon with direct fire into their foxholes, but artillery fire soon stopped the attack.

Kesselring sent a critical letter to Mackensen after the day's fighting, complaining that the attack had not met his expectations. In an unusually sharp response, Mackensen retorted that the attack had failed due to problems discussed even before the attack, namely:

"the insufficient training of the troops, and the young replacements who are not prepared to meet Allied troops in battle. Due to this the Army will be unable to wipe out the beachhead with the troops on hand. The tactics that have been employed, namely to reduce the bridgehead

GIs of the 1st Special Service Force attack a farmhouse during a raid near Ceretto Alto on 14 April 1944.

gradually by concentrated attacks by several divisions, cannot be continued much longer. Now tactics must be established to enable us to meet the eventual large-scale enemy attack from the beachhead with adequate numbers of troops and supplies."

Kesselring responded at 1840 hours, noting that the weather predictions had proven wrong and that the unexpected rain had so drenched the battlefield that Panzer operations were impossible. As a result, he ordered a halt to all major attacks except for small raids to keep the Allies off balance. Losses on 1 March had been 1,374 for no gains whatsoever. The Allies responded the following day with heavy air attacks including 351 heavy bomber sorties dropping tons of fragmentation bombs on German positions around the beachhead.

German casualties on the Anzio front were about 29,000 through the end of the third offensive in late February which included 5,500 killed, 17,500 wounded and 4,500 captured. The German losses were higher than the Allied losses, and the infantry companies were particularly hard hit. German combat units received fewer replacements than comparable Allied units and the replacements were generally of poorer quality than in 1943, with particular shortages among NCOs and junior officers. The replacement problems in the Wehrmacht would only continue to grow worse through 1944.

STALEMATE ALONG THE BEACHHEAD

The collapse of the third German offensive against the beachhead marked the turn of the tide in the Anzio campaign. Kesselring concluded that no further resources would be available from other theaters, and so further large scale operations against Anzio were pointless. Kesselring sent his chief of staff, Gen Siegfried Westphal, to personally tell Hitler "the unvarnished truth" that Army Group C was now forced to go over to the defensive in Italy after the horrible casualties in February. After Westphal briefed Hitler on 6 March, the chief of the high command, Wilhelm Keitel, told him, "You were lucky; if we old fools had said even half as much the Führer would have had us hanged!" Hitler was still

Pvt. Edward Wall of the 1st SSF following a raid along the Strada Litoranea on 15 April 1944. Wall was formerly with the 4th Rangers, but like the rest of the unit was transferred to the 1st SSF following the disbanding of Darby's Rangers; therefore he does not wear the usual 1st SSF insignia. (NARA)

A staged photo of Sgt. Maurice Parker of the 1st SSF with a pair of German prisoners on 15 April 1944. The officer to the left was a company commander with Jäger Regt. 741 of the 114th Jäger Division. (NARA)

suspicious, but finally calmed down after a succession of officers from the Anzio front were brought to him and told much the same story of the horrific losses and the staggering blows of Allied artillery. Hitler advised Kesselring to pay more attention to the forgotten lessons of 1918.

Kesselring instructed the 14th Army to establish firm defensive positions, and the best of its battered divisions were pulled out of the line for rest and refitting. Panzer Division Hermann Göring was sent to Livorno (Leghorn) for rebuilding and the 114th Jäger Division elsewhere on the Adriatic. The 26th Panzer Division and 29th Panzergrenadier Division were pulled back towards Rome for reconstruction and to serve as the Army Group C reserve. Replacements were sent to the remaining infantry units, including two battalions of Italian troops from the new RSI armed forces. On paper, the 14th Army continued to grow in strength as OKW reinforced the Italian theater in anticipation of an Allied spring offensive. The 14th Army reached a strength of over 135,000 troops by mid-March compared to about 90,000 in mid-February. But the 14th Army strength was somewhat illusory as several of these divisions were earmarked for transfer to France or the Russian front and were simply in Italy for training and refitting, not for local combat employment. The increased paper strength tempted Mackensen to start another attack on the beachhead on 29 March, but since Kesselring refused to commit the 26th Panzer Division and 29th Panzergrenadier Division, Mackensen realized that such an attack would most probably be futile. The attack was therefore at first postponed, and then on 10 April 1943 it was abandoned altogether.

The Allies also used March to reorganize. The British 56th Division left and was replaced by the 5th Division. The 1st Division remained but

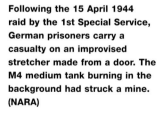

Following the 15 April 1944 raid by the 1st Special Service, German prisoners carry a casualty on an improvised stretcher made from a door. The M4 medium tank burning in the background had struck a mine. (NARA)

Among the secret weapons used against Allied transports in Anzio harbor was the Neger manned torpedo operated by K-Flotilla 175. A massed attack by 17 Neger submarines was made on the night of 20–21 April, and four were lost to US sub-chasers. (NARA)

In anticipation of Operation *Buffalo*, the remainder of the 1st Armored Division was moved into the beachhead to assist in the assault and here some of the division's M4 tanks are seen unloading from an LST. (NARA)

its battered 24th Guards Brigade was replaced by the 18th Brigade. All of the Commando units were withdrawn as were the US paratrooper units. The US 34th Division arrived and took over the 3rd Division sector which went into reserve. By the end of March, the VI Corps had the equivalent of six full divisions in the beachhead, significantly outnumbering the German 14th Army. As in the case of Wehrmacht, the Allies planned several offensive operations for March and April, but none of them came into effect.

The frontline infantry on both sides endured the remorseless agony of stalemate in wretched conditions. The Anzio front in March and April 1944 was reminiscent of a quiet front in World War I. Both sides exchanged artillery fire and conducted small raids to capture prisoners. The entrenchment extended into the rear area of the beachhead since it was so vulnerable to German artillery fire. Indeed, the field hospital area

One of the more curious innovations for Operation *Buffalo* developed by the commander of the 3rd Division was the "battle-sled" consisting of two trains with six sleds each to permit a tank to tow 12 infantrymen behind the tank with some degree of safety. One platoon was moved forward about two miles by tanks of the 751st Tank Battalion near Conca, but the infantry were extremely uncomfortable in the sleds due to the heavy dust and exhaust fumes behind the tanks. (NARA)

An M4 medium tank of the 751st Tank Battalion operating near Cisterna on 9 May 1944 in support of the 3rd Division.

was shelled so often that it was dubbed "Hell's Half-Mile." This period of stalemate was called "the big war of small battles" by the US commanders, an endless series of small skirmishes and raids with few territorial gains, but a continuing toll of infantry casualties. Besides the artillery, the Luftwaffe continued sporadic attacks. One of the most feared weapons was the "butterfly bomb", a cluster bomb that dropped a large number of smaller anti-personnel munitions. While trenches were an adequate defense against normal fragmentation bombs, the butterfly bomb scattered its payload over a wide area, and the small bomblets could find their way into trenches and dugouts with fatal results.

In spite of the lack of major combat actions, the Allied units and the Wehrmacht each suffered a further 10,000 casualties from early March to late May prior to the Allied offensive. The beachhead was located in the marshy coastal plains, which had a high water table. In most sectors, the infantry quickly encountered water when digging trenches. The sodden conditions, exacerbated by winter and spring rain, led to widespread

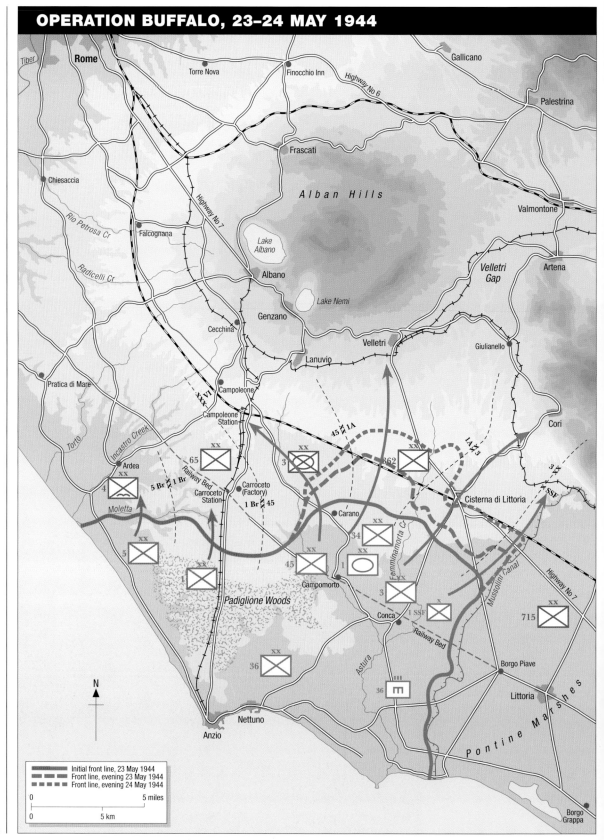

Rome

Tiber

Torre Nova

Finocchio Inn

Gallicano

Highway No 6

Palestrina

Frascati

Chiesaccia

Highway No 7

Alban Hills

Valmontone

Rio Petrosa Cr

Falcognana

Lake Albano

Radicelli Cr

Albano

Lake Nemi

Velletri Gap

Artena

Genzano

Cecchina

Velletri

Giulianello

Lanuvio

Pratica di Mare

Campoleone

XX VI

Cori

Campoleone Station

45 X 1A

1A X 3

Ardea

65

3

362

XX

Torto

Incastro Creek

Railway Bed

5 Br X 1 Br

Carroceto (Factory)

Carroceto Station

1 Br X 45

Carano

Cisterna di Littoria

X SSF

Moletta

4

5

34

1

45

3

Padiglione Woods

Campomorto

Femminamorta Cr

1 SSF

Conca

Railway Bed

715

Mussolini Canal

Highway No 7

36

Astura

36

Borgo Piave

Littoria

N

Nettuno

Anzio

Pontine Marshes

Borgo Grappa

	Initial front line, 23 May 1944
	Front line, evening 23 May 1944
	Front line, evening 24 May 1944

0   5 miles

0   5 km

trenchfoot, as well as outbreaks of malaria, and other diseases. Indeed, Allied non-combat casualties, totaling 37,000, exceeded the combat casualties. Allied combat casualties in the Anzio beachhead up to the late May offensive totaled about 30,000, including 4,400 killed, 18,000 wounded and 6,800 captured. Of these, US units suffered 2,800 killed, 11,000 wounded and 2,400 prisoners. Although the US units suffered a greater number of casualties than the British, British losses were proportionately higher, about 27 percent of strength compared to 17 percent due to the decimation of the 1st Division in February.

OPERATION *BUFFALO*, 23 MAY 1944

Allied planning for the spring offensives included four scenarios for the Anzio breakout. Operation *Turtle* was intended to be a lunge for Rome along the shortest route: straight up the Via Anziate to the junction with Highway 7 to Rome. Needless to say, this was viewed by most of the troops in the beachhead as one of the stupidest plans, since this was the very route that had cost so many lives over the past few months, and the route most heavily defended by the Germans. Operation *Crawdad*, as its name implies, was an attack along the seacoast to the northwest. Although a short distance to Rome, it was not the most practical as this area, the Pratica di Mare, was full of tidal marshes which inhibited the use of tanks. Operation *Grasshopper* was an attack in the opposite direction from the right flank down the coast to the south. This was actually intended as a contingency operation to support a Fifth Army attack from the Gustav line, and was not seriously considered except as an emergency back-up. The final plan, Operation *Buffalo*, was aimed at rupturing the German lines near Cisterna, and then thrusting to the northeast to the Alban hills and the Velletri gap. This plan had several desirable features. The Cisterna axis was not as heavily defended by the Germans as the Via

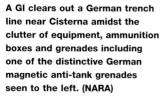
A GI clears out a German trench line near Cisterna amidst the clutter of equipment, ammunition boxes and grenades including one of the distinctive German magnetic anti-tank grenades seen to the left. (NARA)

A GI engages German troops with a water-cooled Browning .30cal. machine gun with an M10 3in GMC tank destroyer in the background near Fondi on 21 May 1944.

German prisoners are escorted to the rear following the break-out operations by the 36th Division near Cisterna on 25 May 1944. (NARA)

Anziate since it did not lead directly to Rome. However, it did offer access to the main Highway 6 leading from Cassino to Rome, which was the main supply route for the German 10th Army. By cutting Highway 6, the Anzio operation could substantially facilitate the attack from Cassino by threatening the main German retreat route. In the end, it was this plan that was selected. However, activation of the plan depended on the rupture of the Gustav line, codenamed Operation *Diadem*. Reinforcement of the Anzio beachhead in early May included the final combat command of the 1st Armored Division, unifying the division in Italy for the first time, and on 22 May the 36th Division arrived in Anzio bringing the strength of VI Corps to seven divisions.

By late spring, Kesselring faced the threat of three simultaneous offensives in several possible locations in the 10th Army sector around

Troops of the US 3rd Division watch as an M4 medium tank drives past during the break-out operation near Cisterna in late May 1944. (NARA)

A company of s.Pz.Jäger Abt. 653 deployed the Elefant 88mm heavy tank destroyers during the Anzio fighting. This example from the 1st Company was captured by US forces in May 1944 and is currently at the Ordnance Museum at Aberdeen Proving Ground in Maryland. (MHI)

Cassino and the Garigliano river, the Ortona front on the Adriatic coast and the 14th Army sector facing the Anzio beachhead. Kesselring was also plagued by very poor intelligence, especially compared to the exceptionally fine efforts by the Allied intelligence organizations. In spite of the considerable movement inherent in reorienting the Fifth and Eight Armies for Operation *Diadem*, Kesselring was none the wiser. Luftwaffe intelligence gathering had collapsed due to the increasing strength of Allied air power over Italy, and German signals intelligence was poor. In such circumstances, Allied deception efforts found fertile ground, and the German planners were led astray to think that the main Allied thrust would be directed up Highway 7 along the coast instead of

Although the I/Pz.Regt. 4 with its new Panther tanks was first committed to the Anzio sector in February 1944, the battalion was held in reserve and saw little fighting during Operation *Fischfang*. This Befelspanzer command tank, one of three in the battalion, was lost on 25 May 1944 near San Giovanni Incarico and is being inspected by some curious GIs. (NARA)

further inland where it was actually aimed. Kesselring was also convinced that the Allies were planning another amphibious end run, probably closer to Rome, a viewpoint that was fostered by a very active and successful Allied deception plan. When Operation *Diadem* began, the 10th Army commander, Vietinghoff, and one of the principal corps commanders, Senger und Etterlin, were away in Germany, along with several key staff officers.

The US Fifth Army built up its strength along the Garigliano river on the coast, while the British Eighth Army took over the Cassino front immediately inland. The Allied plan for Italy was a sequential series of offensives and Operation *Diadem* began on the night of 11–12 May 1944. The Fifth Army broke through on the Garigliano front after three days of fighting and the Eighth Army overwhelmed the Cassino defenses after a week of heavy fighting, breaking open the Gustav line defenses in front of the Liri Valley.

Clark's original plan was to transfer two divisions, the 85th and 88th Divisions, into the Anzio beachhead after the Gustav line had been ruptured to reinforce Operation *Buffalo*. However, the advance from the Gustav line was so rapid that this seemed unnecessary. The focus of Operation *Buffalo* was the 3rd Infantry Division, passing through the 34th Division front. The attack aimed for Valmontone and Highway 6 with a parallel advance by the 1st Armored Division against Velletri in the Alban hills, to defend the left flank of the 3rd Division. The 1st Special Service Force (SSF) would be committed along the 3rd Division's right flank, but this area was expected to be less vigorously defended in view of the rapid advance by the Fifth Army into this sector.

Truscott's challenge was to prepare his forces for the break-out without alerting the Germans to their actual direction. This required a complicated scheme of camouflage and deception, made all the more difficult by the ease with which the Germans could observe all the details of the Allied beachhead from their perch in the Alban hills. The most difficult deception involved the tanks of Harmon's 1st Armored Division. A scheme was developed in the weeks before the break-out to stage evening tank raids along the front. A few tanks would rush

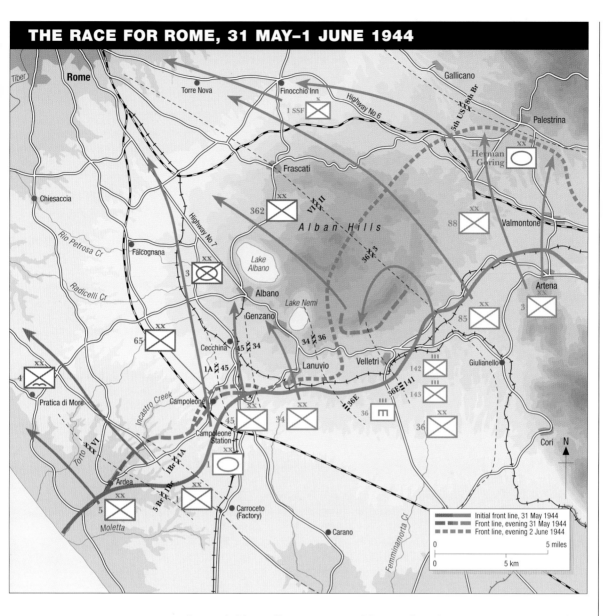

forward, blast off some ammunition against German positions and then pull back. After a few weeks of this, it became routine and the Germans attributed it to the stir-crazy Americans having nothing better to do with their tanks. What Harmon was doing was to use the routine of the tank raids to move his tanks into the attack sector, and then camouflage them while waiting for the attack to begin. Elsewhere, inflatable Sherman tank dummies were positioned in areas away from the Cisterna axis to make up for the missing tanks.

When Operation *Diadem* began on 11–12 May, Kesselring was forced to decide whether or not to commit Mackensen's 14th Army reserves in an attempt to buttress the 10th Army front. He decided it was worth the risk, thereby denuding Mackensen of significant reserves to resist an expected offensive from Anzio. The German defense was further weakened by a flawed intelligence assessment of expected Allied plans. Kesselring was convinced that the Allies would stage another

German columns are seen evacuating through Rome in early June 1944. A bus is being used as an ambulance, and a SdKfz 7 artillery tractor is towing a 150mm sFH 18 heavy field howitzer. (MHI)

amphibious operation, most likely near the mouth of the Tiber river closer to Rome such as the long-threatened attack on Civitavecchia. As a result, units were tied down in a coastal defense role to the west of Rome. Secondly, Kesselring believed that the main Allied attack out of Anzio would pass along the most direct route to Rome, down the Via Anziate and through the heavily contested "Factory." As a result, the best 14th Army units, notably the 3rd Panzergrenadier Division and the 65th Infantry Division were positioned there while the 362nd Infantry Division weakly guarded the extended Cisterna front opposite the actual Allied break-out route.

Operation *Buffalo* kicked off with a 45-minute preparatory artillery barrage at 0545 hours on 23 May along the Cisterna front. The extensive German minefields and obstacles caused significant casualties among the advancing US tanks, but the pace of the attack stayed on schedule. By the end of the day, 86 tanks and tank destroyers had been lost, mainly to mines. The 1st SSF cut Highway 7 below Cisterna before noon, and the 1st Armored Division solidly punched through the 362nd Infantry Division and passed the Cisterna–Campoleone railroad by evening. The offensive devastated the German units in its path with the 362nd Infantry Division losing half its combat strength and the 715th Infantry Division having two of its regiments battered in the fighting. Mackensen was unable to shift forces from the more heavily defended sectors to the west since the British 1st and 5th Divisions and the US 45th Division were also attacking in their sectors. Cisterna was encircled on 24 May and the town fell to the 3rd Division on 25 May after two days of intense fighting. A journalist entering the shattered town compared it to the lunar landscapes of World War I such as Ypres. The 1st Armored Division raced to the northern side of the Velletri gap, capturing the town of Cori. On 26 May, the 1st Armored Division advanced to within two miles of Velletri while reconnaissance units of the 3rd Division raced ahead to the outskirts of Artena, three miles from Valmontone and Highway 6. After three days of intensive action, the pace of the VI Corps slowed. US casualties had been high, exceeding 4,000, but German losses were far greater, totaling 4,838 prisoners alone. Harmon prepared a special task force, TF Howze, led by cavalryman Ernie Howze, as his exploitation force to race to the highway. In its first outing on the afternoon of 25 May, TF Howze blocked one of the German escape routes via the Cori–Giulianello road, and shot up several German motorized columns. The Allied air units joined in the fray, claiming to have destroyed 645 tanks and vehicles along the main roads while damaging a further 446.

In an entirely different direction, the long siege of the Anzio beachhead formally ended on the morning of 25 May 1944, when troops of the 36th Engineers linked up with the 48th Engineers of US II Corps near Borgo Grappa on the Mediterranean coast southeast of Anzio. The event was restaged later in the morning with Mark Clark present along with a horde of photographers.

With the German defenses in front of Anzio broken wide open, on 25 May, Gen Mark Clark began to reconsider the *Buffalo* plan. Clark was obsessed by the desire for the US Fifth Army to liberate Rome. He shared Churchill's view that this was the glittering prize of the Italian campaign, arguably the only prize. Clark knew full well that once the Normandy campaign began in a few weeks, that Italy would become a backwater. The US Seventh Army was already being prepared in Italy for an amphibious invasion of southern France as soon as enough amphibious transport was available. He was also troubled to the point of paranoia by Alexander's reference to the Liri valley as "the only route" to Rome, worrying him that it would be the British Eighth Army that would be given the honor of capturing Rome, with VI Corps simply facilitating their approach by seizing Valmontone. In reality, the Eighth Army, now under Gen Leese since Montgomery's departure to command ground forces in Normandy, was still stalled to the south by German resistance.

In one of the most controversial acts in an already controversial campaign, Clark chose to halt the VI Corps attack towards Valmontone and reorient it along the Alban hills towards Rome, thereby switching from the *Buffalo* plan to the *Turtle* plan. This clearly defied his instructions from Alexander. Clark considered three options for the VI

An M10 3in GMC tank destroyer fires pointblank at a target in the suburbs of Rome on 4 June 1944. (NARA)

An M10 tank destroyer battalion drives past the Colosseum on 5 June 1944 following the capture of the city. (MHI)

Corps on 25 May 1944. The first was to continue Operation *Buffalo* as planned, aimed at reaching Highway 6 and cutting the main supply road of the retreating German 10th Army. The other main option was to redirect VI Corps from the planned northward drive towards Valmontone, and reorient it northwestward along the base of the Alban hills and towards Rome. Since there were five more uncommitted

divisions in VI Corps, this route seemed like it might be the fastest

A US column led by a pair of jeeps passes through Rome on 5 June 1944 after the fighting had quietened down. (NARA)

means to reach Rome. The third alternative was to attempt advances along both routes, allowing the 1st Armored Division and 3rd Division to continue on to Valmontone and then to Rome along Highway 6 while the remainder of the corps moved in the Albano–Rome direction to the west of the Alban hills. Clark chose the second option, reorienting the entire attack axis to the northwest, apparently the shortest route to Rome. Clark's decision infuriated his subordinate commanders, Ernie Harmon of the 1st Armored Division and "Iron Mike" O'Daniel of the 3rd Division. Truscott personally visited Clark to protest the order. Clark claimed he was merely using a commander's prerogative to exploit success and that cutting Highway 6 was no guarantee of bagging the German 10th Army since there were alternative routes. Truscott bitterly remarked afterwards "to be the first in Rome was poor compensation for this lost opportunity".

What Clark had overlooked was the possibility that the shortest route was not necessarily the quickest route. While the German defenses in front of the 34th Division had been split wide open, Mackensen's 14th Army was continuing to hold the Via Anziate and the Caesar defensive line across the Alban hills. There were three good German divisions blocking the Via Anziate, and the formidable artillery and defensive positions in the Caesar line. The route to Valmontone was blocked by parts of the Caesar line, but the actual troop strength was low and the intended defense of the Velletri gap by Panzer Division Hermann Göring was far from complete due to the heavy losses suffered during the division's road march from Leghorn. In addition, it would take the 1st Armored Division and 3rd Division nearly two days to reorient their units for the abrupt shift in plans. The switch from Operation *Buffalo* to Operation *Turtle* was officially ordered by Gen Clark on 26 May 1944. Although the 1st Armored Division was first assigned to continue its attack towards Velletri, it was repositioned to the west on 28 May to assist the 45th Division to punch through the tough German defenses along the Via Anziate.

The dissension within the rank of senior American commanders was matched by turmoil within the German high command. Kesselring complained to Mackensen about his lack of attention to the Cisterna axis after the Americans had broken through. The main German defenses had been oriented along the Via Anziate and along the so called C-Position, or Caesar line, blocking approaches to Rome via the lowlands on either side of the Alban hills. Kesselring was also infuriated by Mackensen's delay in releasing the 29th Panzergrenadier Division to the 10th Army, and by the time it arrived on the Gustav line it had no time to prepare defenses and was smashed. Mackensen did not appreciate how few reserves Kesselring controlled, and how vital he considered the need to quickly shift the reserve divisions in a time of crisis. Kesselring became

US infantry march through Rome on 5 July 1944.

so aggravated by Mackensen's actions that he sacked him several days later on 4 June.

For three days, the VI Corps pushed out of the Anzio beachhead past familiar ground such as "The Factory" and reached the outskirts of Campoleone Station and Lanuvio. By this time, the US II Corps had advanced up the coast from the Garigliano river. The 3rd Division and the 1st SSF in the Velletri gap were turned over to II Corps, as was the assignment to push on to Valmontone and Highway 6. In spite of these advances, the German defenses to the west of the Alban hills continued to hold firm, and by 30 May, the American advance had stalled. Instead of the disorganized, panicked formations facing the VI Corps on 25 May in the Velletri gap, the units were again facing determined resistance by well-entrenched German troops. Furthermore, the shift in emphasis had given Kesselring the time to reinforce the vulnerable Velletri gap to cover the retreat of the 10th Army towards Rome. Allied casualties were quickly mounting, reaching over 5,100 from the start of Operation *Buffalo* to the end of May.

On 30 May, prospects suddenly brightened. The 36th Division was being shifted into the Velletri area to take over from the 34th Division, and the commander, Maj. Gen Fred Walker, had a hunch that the quiet sector in the Alban hills might offer some tactical opportunity. Walker dispatched a reconnaissance patrol into the Alban hills near Velletri and found an undefended corridor along the corps boundary between the 1st Fallschirmjäger Corps and the 76th Panzer Corps. Truscott was at first skeptical but on visiting the division on 30 May, Walker convinced him that he could slip one or more regiments over the center of the Alban hills. Late on the evening of 30 May, two regiments of the 36th Division began ascending the slopes of the Alban hills and by dawn, the two regiments were deep into the flanks of the two German corps and in control of Mount Artemisio. Realizing the significance of the penetration, Truscott ordered the ever-versatile 36th Engineers to bulldoze a path to permit vehicles to ascend behind the infantry to provide logistical support. German counterattacks were ineffective.

Clark had yet another change of heart and decided that after all, the route through Valmontone might be the quickest approach to Rome. A renewed effort by the 3rd Division closed off the town, and even as Kesselring was attempting to rush the 90th Panzergrenadier Division to its defense, the garrison there surrendered on 1 June 1944. The German 14th Army continued to resist to the west of the Alban hills but by the evening of 2 June, the 36th Division was advancing over the Alban hills towards Rome, and the II Corps had pushed through the Velletri gap and Valmontone and were about to sever Highway 6. Kesselring was well aware that the defense of the Caesar line was now completely compromised and that breaches were occurring with alarming frequency all along the front. Mackensen ordered a withdrawal of the 14th Army from the area south of Rome on the evening of 2-3 June except for rearguards. Having delayed as long as he could, on 3 June Kesselring declared Rome an open city and authorized the withdrawal of all units of Army Group C to the next defense line north of Rome except for rearguard units intended to delay the American advance. Hitler had already accepted the likelihood of Rome falling, and his senior commanders had convinced him that the new Gothic line north of Rome offered better prospects for a prolonged defense of northern Italy. It was the only major capital in 1944–45 where Hitler did not demand "a fight to the death".

Lead elements of the VI Corps reached the outskirts of Rome in the early morning of Sunday 4 June 1944. Tanks from Task Force Howze, and units of the Special Service Force ran into German rearguard units, and a nine-hour battle ensued as the Germans tried to delay the American advance long enough to extract all their units out of the city. Across the front, there was a race to be the first unit into Rome. Units of the 1st Armored Division and the 36th Division tussled for control of Highway 7, forcing Truscott to clear up the traffic jam by ordering Walker's division to stick to his assigned routes and clear Highway 7 for the tanks.

By early afternoon, large portions of the 1st Armored Division and 36th Division had reached the southern suburbs, but German rearguards and an unwillingness to cause extensive civilian casualties limited the American penetration into the city. After dark, the US units began infiltrating into the center of the city, now mostly abandoned by the Germans. Full scale movement through the city did not occur until 5 June, and even then, some units were still engaged in firefights with scattered German rearguards. Other units of the Fifth Army continued up the coast, so that by the end of the day, the Fifth Army were positioned from Rome all the way to the sea along the Tiber river.

The Fifth Army's glory was short-lived. Clark was able to bask in glory for one day, but on 6 June, the Allies landed in Normandy, removing the limelight from the Italian theater once and for all.

THE CAMPAIGN IN RETROSPECT

The most astute assessment of the Anzio campaign came from the distinguished commander of the French expeditionary force in Italy, General Alphonse Juin: "Once again we have run into one of those stumbling blocks of coalition warfare: the Allies cannot come to an agreement and co-ordinate their efforts. Questions of prestige are shaping events, each one wanting to make the entry into Rome. History will not fail to pass severe sentence."

The conduct of the Anzio campaign offers ample opportunity for criticism of senior Allied leadership. Churchill's dogged advocacy of the Anzio landing was marred by an amateur enthusiasm, wishful thinking about the likely German response, and bullying of the officers who raised objections about the plan's obvious flaws. Had the operation been conducted as originally intended, a tactical outflanking maneuver close enough to the Gustav line to force a German withdrawal, it might have succeeded. But Churchill and Clark were too blinded by the glory of liberating Rome to be content with a mere tactical victory. While Lucas' conduct of the Anzio operation in the first week was hardly flawless, the criticism that he should have seized the Alban hills is unwarranted as VI Corps lacked the resources and the Germans were not foolish enough to be intimidated by a bluff. A more valid criticism is that neither Lucas nor the Fifth Army planners gave enough thought to what would constitute a viable defensive line for the bridgehead, and so overlooked the need to seize Campoleone and Cisterna at the earliest feasible moment. Lucas was a scapegoat for the initial failure at Anzio, while the architects of the scheme including Churchill and Clark, continued to bluster about the need for more action to redeem an inherently flawed plan.

Clark's actions in late May on the approaches to Rome have rightly spawned their own set of controversies. On the one hand, Clark's focus on Rome as being the prime strategic objective of the Fifth Army is less debatable than his decisions of how to attain that goal. The prime architect of the Anzio operation, Winston Churchill, had made it abundantly clear that the strategic mission was to seize Rome, and Clark certainly needed little additional encouragement to carry out this assignment. Alexander's diffident command style gave Clark little reason to forsake this mission and concentrate instead on trapping the retreating German 10th Army. But it was not a choice of one or the other. With the resources at hand, Clark could have exacted a heavier price from the retreating 10th Army by continuing Operation *Buffalo* a few days longer, and doing so would have facilitated the Rome mission rather than diverting resources from it. Clark's decision to switch from Operation *Buffalo* to *Turtle*, thereby sending VI Corps into the face of the stiffest German defenses, is a damning testimony of his flawed tactical understanding.

In contrast to the blunders of Allied commanders, Kesselring's conduct of operations in Italy was outstanding at the tactical and operational level. Some German officers have questioned the strategic dimensions of the Italian campaign, such as whether it was worth committing so many divisions to so peripheral a theater. It can certainly be argued that Hitler fell into the Allied trap, and continued to feed divisions into Italy when they should have been reserved for France or the Russian front. What was also noteworthy about the Italian campaign was Hitler's relative lack of interference in Kesselring's conduct of the operations compared to the dysfunctional and disastrous command situation several months later in France.

The actual conduct of the Anzio campaign was a remarkable demonstration of the grim perseverance of the British, American, and German infantry in the face of appalling battlefield conditions. Due to the terrain, the Anzio battlefield was dominated by artillery, more akin to the Western Front in World War I than to the fighting in France later in the year where armor played a more decisive role.

Anzio had unexpected consequences for operations in Normandy several months later. Kesselring later argued that the lessons learned by the Allies at Anzio were instrumental in the victory in the West later in 1944–45. This may be a bit of an exaggeration, but the Allied navies continued to hone their skills in amphibious operations with the Anzio landings. The Allied air forces' performance at Anzio, while good, still had rough edges that needed ironing out. One of the frequently overlooked consequences of Anzio was the distorting effect it had on German perceptions of Allied operational aims in Normandy. At first, the Germans assessed Anzio for what it really was – a failed gamble to quickly seize Rome. But the dogged Allied efforts to keep the beachhead intact months after this mission had failed led the Germans to divine more sinister motives about its mission. OKW planners became convinced that Anzio was an economy-of-force operation intended to draw off large numbers of German divisions for a relatively modest Allied commitment. This assessment predisposed the Germans to view the Normandy landing as a similar economy-of-force mission aimed at drawing off German divisions until the main thrust came on the Pas de Calais, a viewpoint reinforced by successful Allied deception operations. While Anzio alone can hardly be credited with the German strategic misperceptions in June 1944, the distorted echoes of Operation *Shingle* continued to resonate in Berlin, long after Allied commanders had dismissed Anzio as, at best, a pyrrhic victory.

THE BATTLEFIELD TODAY

Anzio is one of those World War II battles that both sides would like to forget. In spite of the enormous sacrifice of British, German, and US troops, there was little fame or glory in the agony of Anzio. It is hard to even find a mention of Anzio in tourist guides to Italy. In view of its proximity to Rome, the area was quickly rebuilt after the war and few traces of the fighting remain. The most prominent reminders of the battle are the two large military cemeteries, the American cemetery immediately to the north of Nettuno and the British military cemetery north of Anzio along the current Route No. 207 to Albano. The main German cemetery is located away from Anzio to the northwest nearer Rome. Other signs of the battle have gradually been lost. The last of the Italian and German seacoast fortifications were removed in 1976. Even the names have been changed to erase old memories. The Mussolini canal, the southeastern edge of the Anzio beach head in 1944, was renamed Moscarello after the war. Some small traces of the fighting can still be found, a few battle-scarred pillars at the Isola Bella farm on the road to Cisterna, the abutments of "The Flyover". But most of the buildings damaged in the fighting have been rebuilt and few traces of the war remain. "The Factory" has resumed life as the town of Aprilia. It has been reconstructed though some buildings that existed before the fighting such as the San Antonio chapel were not rebuilt. Other towns such as Cisterna, heavily damaged by the fighting, have also been thoroughly rebuilt. A very useful guide for readers wishing to visit the battlefield is Issue 52 (1986) of *After the Battle* magazine, devoted to Anzio.

Other traces of the battle remain, though in more distant locales. The K5E railroad gun, known to the Germans as *Leopold* and to the GIs as "Anzio Annie" was sent back to Aberdeen Proving Ground, Maryland for technical evaluation in 1944. It still remains as one of the most awesome and popular exhibits at the US Army Ordnance Museum at APG.

FURTHER READING

An excellent starting place for more detailed reading about Anzio are the official histories. The US side of the story is handled in the two volumes of the US Army "Green Book" series by Blumenson and Fischer. Likewise, the British side is well covered in the official history mentioned below by the team headed by Brigadier C. Molony. On the German side, a semi-official history was prepared after the war by reconstructing and translating the German 14th Army diary into an English language account titled *The German Operation at Anzio*. This is not widely available, but the author found a copy at the US Army Military History Institute at Carlisle Barracks, Pennsylvania. Additional detail on the German operations at Anzio can be found in the several studies in the Foreign Military Studies series which were prepared by senior German commanders after the war at the behest of the US Army's Office of Military History. The author consulted the collection at the Military History Institute, but other collections of these documents exist at the National Archives and Records Administration (NARA) at College Park, Maryland and other US government historical facilities. In view of the controversy over Anzio, there are numerous accounts of the battle in English, and the following list covers those that the author found especially helpful or interesting. Not listed here are the many unit histories that bear on the campaign.

Blumenson, Martin, *Anzio: The Gamble that Failed*, Lippincott, 1963. A brisk, popular account by one of the stars of the wartime US Army historians.

Blumenson, Martin et al., *Command Decisions*, Harcourt, Brace, 1959. Prepared in conjunction with the Chief of Military History of the US Army, this study contains an excellent essay by Blumenson on the controversies surrounding the Anzio plans.

Blumenson, Martin, *Salerno to Cassino*, US Army, 1969. The first of the two volumes of the US Army "Green Book" series dealing with Anzio from the landings through the end of the German counter-offensives in February.

Bowditch, John et. al., *Anzio Beachhead*, US Army, 1947. This is the first US Army study of the Anzio battle, subsequently reprinted several times, and worth the price for the excellent and numerous maps alone.

Clark, Mark, *Calculated Risk*, Harper, 1950. Clark's autobiography offers a rather pallid account of the key decisions and controversies about Anzio.

D'Este, Carlo, *Fatal Decision: Anzio and the Battle for Rome*, HarperCollins, 1991. A superb new account by one of the new generation of American military historians.

Fisher, Ernest Jr., *Cassino to the Alps*, US Army, 1977. The second of the two US Army "Green Book" volumes covering the breakout operations from Anzio.

Higgins, Trumball, *Soft Underbelly: The Anglo-American Controversy over the Italian Campaign 1939–1945*, Macmillan, 1968. A fine academic history of the controversies amongst the Allies over the grand strategy affecting Italy.

Kesselring, A., *The Memoirs of Field Marshal Kesselring*, William Kimber, 1953. The principal German commander's view of the strategic aspects of Anzio, though not as detailed as one might wish.

Hinsley, F.H., *British Intelligence in the Second World War*, Cambridge, 1993. A fine multi-volume history provides a clear explanation of what the Allied commanders knew, and when they knew it, based on various forms of intelligence gathering, including Enigma.

Kurowski, Franz, *Battleground Italy 1943–1945: The German Armed Forces in the Battle for the Boot*, Federowicz, 2003. An anecdotal, popular, and somewhat disjointed account worth tracking down due to the paucity of accounts from the German perspective.

Molony, C. et al, *History of the Second World War: The Mediterranean and Middle East, Vol. V*, HMSO, 1973. This is the British official history and done to a high standard. This volume covers the period up to the end of March 1944 and Vol. VI continues the account beyond the liberation of Rome.

Morison, Samuel E., *Sicily–Salerno–Anzio: January 1943–June 1944*, Little, Brown, 1954. This is volume 9 in the semi-official history of the US Navy in World War II and a very useful account of the naval aspects of the Anzio operation.

Starr, Chester, *From Salerno to the Alps: A History of the Fifth Army 1943–45*, Infantry Journal, 1948. A semi-official one-volume history of the Fifth Army, available now in a Battery Press reprint, and a more accessible alternative to the multi-volume Fifth Army history.

Truscott, Lucian, *Command Missions*, Dutton, 1954. An account by the second of the VI Corps commanders at Anzio examining some of the controversial decisions by Clark and Alexander.

INDEX

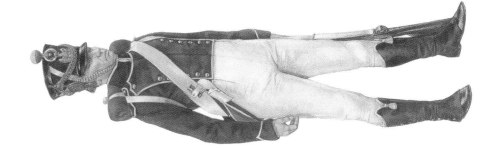

FIND OUT MORE ABOUT OSPREY

❑ Please send me the latest listing of Osprey's publications

❑ I would like to subscribe to Osprey's e-mail newsletter

Title / rank

Name

Address

City / county

Postcode / zip   state / country

e-mail

CAM

I am interested in:

❑ Ancient world
❑ Medieval world
❑ 16th century
❑ 17th century
❑ 18th century
❑ Napoleonic
❑ 19th century

❑ American Civil War
❑ World War 1
❑ World War 2
❑ Modern warfare
❑ Military aviation
❑ Naval warfare

Please send to:

North America:
Osprey Direct , 2427 Bond Street, University Park, IL 60466, USA

UK, Europe and rest of world:
Osprey Direct UK, P.O. Box 140, Wellingborough, Northants, NN8 2FA, United Kingdom

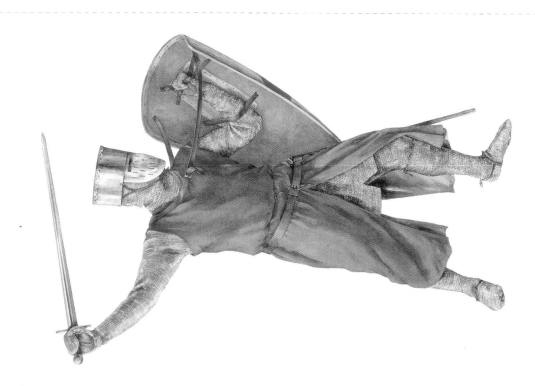

OSPREY
PUBLISHING

www.ospreypublishing.com

call our telephone hotline
for a free information pack

USA & Canada: 1-800-826-6600
UK, Europe and rest of world call:
+44 (0) 1933 443 863

Young Guardsman
Figure taken from *Warrior 22:
Imperial Guardsman 1799–1815*
Published by Osprey
Illustrated by Richard Hook

Knight, c.1190
Figure taken from *Warrior 1: Norman Knight 950 – 1204 AD*
Published by Osprey
Illustrated by Christa Hook

POSTCARD